# The Ultimate Bathroom Reader

*Interesting Stories, Fun Facts and Just Crazy Weird*
*Stuff to Keep You Entertained on the Throne!*

**BILL O'NEILL**

ISBN: 978-1-64845-080-8

# DON'T FORGET YOUR FREE BOOKS

# CONTENTS

# INTRODUCTION

Who doesn't love a bit of random trivia now and then? Or, for that matter, who doesn't enjoy plucking some obscure tidbit of information from the back of their mind and dropping it into conversation?

In simple terms, that is what this book is all about. Collected here are some of the world's most peculiar, astonishing, weird, and wacky facts and anecdotes, covering everything from sports to space travel, movies to medicine, Sherlock Holmes to Shakespeare, and football to pharaohs.

Here you'll find out about the very first word sent over the internet — and what happened to it when the computer it was being sent by, crashed. Here too is the world's most populated river, the world's oldest tallest building, the world's most successful Olympian, and the world's fastest disappearing lake.

Why did the nation of Sudan crash out of the Top 10 largest countries in 2011? Why did everyone at the very first Oscars' ceremony already know who the winners would be? Why did the people of New York riot over the price of flour in 1837? Additionally just how likely are you to be hit by the ball while in the stands of a baseball match?

All of these facts plus hundreds more are listed here, in simple, bite-size chunks — with a few pop quizzes thrown in

1

just to keep your brain ticking over! Who knows what you might pick up if you have a couple of minutes to spare?

# FIRST THINGS FIRST

## Famous Firsts

When it was established by Congress on March 1, 1872, Yellowstone became the first national park in the United States and is considered to be the first in the world.

The first "selfie" was taken in 1839 by a Philadelphia chemist named Robert Cornelius.

The word alphabet derives from *alpha* and *beta*—the first two letters of the Greek alphabet.

The fifth person to decline a Nobel Prize was the French writer and philosopher Jean-Paul Sartre. He turned down the Nobel Prize in Literature in 1964.

The first Christmas tree at the Rockefeller Center in New York was erected in 1931.

In 1989, British explorer Robert Swan became the first person to walk to both the North and South Poles.

The world's first ATM opened on June 27, 1967, at a branch of Barclays Bank in London, England. Reg (Reginald) Varney—a popular sitcom star in England at the time—was the first person to withdraw money from it.

Geologists think the first rocks may have formed on Earth around four billion years ago.

Although George Washington oversaw its construction, he never lived in the White House. The first president to do so was John Adams in 1st November 1800.

On October 4, 1953, Grazio Castellano of Brooklyn, New York, became the first person to roll a perfect ten-pin bowling score of 300 on live television.

The first word ever broadcast over the internet was "LOGIN" by a UCLA student named Charley Kline in 1969. The system he was using crashed after the first two letters, however — so the full word wasn't successfully sent until an hour after he started typing it.

The first banknotes were Chinese. They were introduced sometime during the Tang Dynasty, 618–907.

The first country alphabetically is Afghanistan.

The first Boston Marathon was first held on April 19, 1897. It is the world's oldest marathon competition.

In 2003, UK Prime Minister Tony Blair became the first serving head of state to provide a voice on *The Simpsons*.

On December 6, 1923, Calvin Coolidge became the first president to address the American people over the radio.

# THE MAINE EVENT

## Stories about the State of Maine

Maine is the northernmost state in the North-eastern United States. Maine is the 12th smallest by area, the 9th least populous, and the 13th least densely populated of the 50 U.S. states.

Here are some other things worth knowing about the Pine Tree State.

According to the U.S. Department of Agriculture Forest Service, 89.46% of Maine is forest—more than any other state.

At one point, 95% of all the world's toothpicks were manufactured in Maine. Toothpicks manufactured from wood are no longer in production in Maine.

Ellsworth, Maine, is home to the Telephone Museum (Ellsworth) dedicated to telephones.

According to a study by Swiftkey.com, Mainers are the most positive Americans: they use the thumbs-up emoji more than people from any other state and are the most users of the food emoji at Thanksgiving.

If all of Maine's 3,100 offshore islands are included, then it has a longer total coastline than California at 3,478 miles length.

There are 40 acres of desert just west of Freeport, Maine. Formed by overgrazing and deforestation, the desert isn't made of sand but silt deposited at the end of the last Ice Age.

Stephen King—a famous Mainer, who has set most of his novels in the state—wrote his first novel, *Carrie*, while working as a schoolteacher and cleaner in Bangor.

Maine is the only state to border only one US state. It borders more Canadian territories than it does U.S. states: only New Hampshire lies to the west, but both Québec and New Brunswick lie to the north.

Nine out of ten of all the lobsters caught in American waters are from Maine.

Out of all 50 states, only Alaska has a higher moose population than Maine.

In 1850, Portland, Maine, was home to the world's first chewing gum factory.

There are towns in Maine called China, Lebanon, Peru, Norway, Wales, and Mexico.

Many things have been invented in Maine, from the microwave oven to a zigzag-stitching sewing machine. But one of the state's proudest inventions is also one of its humblest: In 1873, 15-year-old Farmington native Chester Greenwood invented the earmuff. Greenwood was allergic to the woolen winter caps of the time, and so set about patenting what he called an "improvement in ear-mufflers." His design featured a wire headband, two discs of beaver fur, and a unique V-shaped hinge that kept the muffs tight against the head. His design quickly caught on; by the mid-1930s, Maine was producing 400,000 pairs a year. To this day, a celebratory earmuff parade is still held in Greenwood's honor in Farmington every winter.

*"Maine is a joy in the summer. But the soul of Maine is more apparent in the winter."*

**Paul Theroux**

# RAIN & SHINE

## Timeline of strange weather events

It never rains, but it pours. Here are some of the wildest, wettest, and weirdest days in world weather history.

### 535–536: "A MOST DREAD PORTENT"

Historians in ancient Byzantium described "a most dread portent" that fell across the world in CE 535 that was so bad "the sun gave forth its light without brightness" for months on end. Accounts from all across Europe and Asia at the time say much the same thing, and describe a year of late snows and frosts, freezing fogs, droughts, and a prolonged stretch of icy weather lasting long into the following year. It's thought the bizarre conditions were the result of a volcanic eruption somewhere in central Africa.

### 1091: LONDON BRIDGE IS FALLING DOWN

On Friday, October 14, 1091, a huge tornado struck the city of London, England, destroying the original wooden London Bridge and several nearby buildings. Four 26 ft.-long rafters were torn from the roof of a local church and driven into the ground so forcefully that only 4 ft. of them remained visible. Remarkably, there were only two reported fatalities.

## 1816: THE YEAR SUMMER DIDN'T HAPPEN

In April 1815, the Mount Tambora volcano in Indonesia erupted, sending a huge amount of volcanic ash into the Earth's atmosphere. The dust soon spread across the entire Northern Hemisphere, disrupting the world's climate for many months and effectively canceling the summer of the following year. In America and Europe, winter frosts and snowfall persisted long into 1816, killing crops and causing food shortages. In Asia, the annual monsoon season was delayed and worsened, causing huge floods. 1816 ultimately went down in history as "The Year Without A Summer" — although some people at the time preferred to call it "Eighteen-Hundred-and-Frozen-Stiff."

## 1887: SNOW IN CALIFORNIA

Nearly four inches of snow fell in downtown San Francisco on the night of February 5, 1887, which remains a record in the city to this day. The snow was just one part of one of the worst winters in American history.

## 1896: HOT IN THE CITY

One of the United States' worst ever heatwaves lasted for ten days in August 1896. Temperatures in New York City remained above 72°F even at night, and the situation became so dire that police stations were commandeered to hand out ice, and local people were permitted to sleep outdoors in parks. Over 1,500 people in tenements died.

## 1966: RAINING CHAMPION

The world record for rainfall was set on Réunion Island, a tiny French dependency in the southern Indian Ocean, on January 8, 1966. In 24 hours, the island endured 71.8 inches of rain — just shy of 6 ft. in total — during a tropical cyclone.

But the rainiest place on Earth is probably Cherrapunji, India. Cherrapunji holds many of the world's rainfall records. The heaviest rain in a single month happened there – 9,300 millimeters – that's over 360 inches of rainfall.

*"Climate is what we expect. Weather is what we get."*

***Mark Twain***

# XTRA KNOWLEDGE

## Words beginning with "X"

X begins the fewest number of words of any letter in the English language. On average, only around one in every 2,000 English words is an X word. Expand your vocabulary beyond x-ray and xylophone with these excellent X-words.

A xenodochium is a hostel or a room in a house in which strangers are made welcome.

A xiph is a swordfish. (Xiphophorus)

A xenagogue is a tour guide or someone whose job it is to direct strangers.

Xesturgy is the process of polishing something using stones.

Somewhere that is xeric is extremely arid.

A Xanthippe is an ill-tempered shrewish woman. It was the name of the wife of Socrates, who had such a reputation for her foul moods that her name became a byword for a cantankerous woman.

A xerophagous person eats or prefers dry food.

Anything xilinous is made of cotton.

A xystus is a decorative walkway or portico referred to in Roman times.

A xenium is a present given to a houseguest.

A xoanon is a simple carved statue or talisman depicting a god.

A xebec is a three-masted merchant ship, once much used across the Mediterranean.

If you're xanthodontic, then you have yellow teeth.

The Mexican hairless dog is properly known as the xoloitzcuintli (although for brevity, it's usually just called the xolo!)

A friendly relationship between two people from different households or nations would be described as xenial.

Xylographica are woodcut images, engravings and letters.

Transplanting an organ from a non-human donor animal into a human being (like pigs' heart valves) is properly called xenotransplantation.

Something that is xiphoid is sword-shaped.

In his *Dictionary of the English Language* in 1755, the great scholar Dr. Samuel Johnson didn't include any words at all beginning with X. Instead, between W and Y on page 2,308 of his dictionary is a note stating simply, "X is a letter which, though found in Saxon words, begins no word in the English language."

# POP QUIZ!

## GEOGRAPHY

1. The Antarctic Desert is the world's largest desert. What is the second largest?
2. In what Canadian province is Vancouver?
3. What is the only country in the world whose name begins with the letter O?
4. There aren't a thousand islands in the Thousand Islands archipelago. How many are there: 864, 1,264, or 1,864?
5. In what country does the river Nile meet the Mediterranean Sea?
6. The world's tallest waterfall is Angel Falls. In what South American country is it?
7. The island nations of Fiji, Vanuatu, and Nauru all lie in what ocean?
8. What is the capital city of Sweden?
9. The Cook Strait is the stretch of water that divides the two constituent islands of what country?
10. In what European country are the cities of Innsbruck, Salzburg, and Graz?
11. Which English city lies at the mouth of the river Mersey?
12. By surface area, which is the smallest of the five Great Lakes?

13. And by maximum depth, which is the deepest of the five Great Lakes?

14. The countries of Nepal and Bhutan lie almost entirely in what mountain range?

15. Portugal shares a land border with just one other country. Which one?

16. Which of these cities lies the furthest north: London, Prague, Moscow, Tokyo, or Seoul?

17. In 2019, the Republic of Macedonia officially added another word to its name. What is it now called?

18. On what ocean do the coastlines of Uruguay and Argentina stand?

19. Which of these countries does not have a capital city beginning with A: Greece, Ethiopia, Jordan, Turkey, or Cambodia?

20. What is the longest river in Australia called?

# *Answers*

1. Kalahari.
2. British Columbia.
3. Oman.
4. 1,864.
5. Egypt.
6. Venezuela.
7. The Pacific Ocean.
8. Stockholm.
9. New Zealand.
10. Austria.
11. Liverpool.
12. Ontario.
13. Superior.
14. The Himalayas.
15. Spain.
16. Moscow.
17. The Socialist Republic of Macedonia.
18. The Atlantic Ocean.
19. Cambodia (its capital is Phnom Penh).
20. Murray.

# BODY LANGUAGE

## List of body parts named after people

The Achilles tendon at the back of the foot is called that because the hero Achilles is said to have been held by his heel when he was dipped in the River Styx, rendering his entire body invulnerable—all except his heel, of course. From head to toe, here are some more bodily namesakes.

### BROCA'S AREA

Broca's area is a part of the brain's frontal lobe that is responsible for speech production and the interpretation of language. Working in the mid-1800s, the French physician and anatomist Pierre Paul Broca noted that two of his patients who had suffered trauma to roughly the same part of their brain had trouble forming and interpreting words. He rightly concluded that this particular region of the brain's cortex must be responsible for processing language, and the region still bears his name today.

### THE CANALS OF SCHLEMM

It might sound like something you'd expect to find on a map of Venice, but the canals of Schlemm are tiny ducts in the eye that channel the aqueous humor (the watery fluid found inside the eyeball) into the bloodstream. They were named by Friedrich Schlemm, a 19th-century German anatomy professor who also discovered the nerves that control the cornea in 1830.

## BACHMANN'S BUNDLE

Also known as the interatrial tract, Bachmann's bundle is a broad mass of muscle in the middle of the heart connecting the right and left walls of the two atriums. It is named for its discoverer, the German-American physiologist Jean George Bachmann. When your heart beats, an electrical impulse passes through the bundle from right to left, causing the two atriums to contract.

## PURKINJE FIBERS

That electrical impulse that sparks each heartbeat is carried through the muscles of the heart by tiny electrically-motivated cells called Purkinje fibers. They are named for a Czech scientist and anatomist called Jan Evangelista Purkinje, who discovered them in 1839. Although little known today, Purkinje was one of the most famous scientists in 19th-century Europe: Reportedly, anyone wishing to write him from abroad could merely put "Purkinje, Europe" on the envelope and their letter would find its way to him.

## THE ARTERY OF ADAMKIEWICZ

A Polish anatomist named Albert Wojciech Adamkiewicz is the namesake of one of the major blood vessels supplying the spinal cord, known as the artery of Adamkiewicz. Also called the major anterior segmental medullary, in most people, the artery enters the spinal canal from the left side — but in around one in five people, it will enter from the right.

## THE ISLETS OF LANGERHANS

These tiny "islets" are circular masses of hormone-producing cells in the pancreas. Named for their discoverer, the German anatomist Paul Langerhans, they make up just 2% of the entire mass of the pancreas but are immensely important as they produce and secrete insulin, and are used by the body in the metabolism of glucose.

## McBURNEY'S POINT

In 1889, the American surgeon Charles McBurney pinpointed a spot on the right side of the abdomen, roughly halfway between the navel and the topmost point of the hipbone. The point, McBurney explained, was the site of the worst pain experienced by someone suffering from acute appendicitis. Pain in this region is now known as McBurney's Sign and is still used to diagnose appendicitis to this day.

## BABINSKI REFLEX POINT

Another point of the body used in medical diagnosis is located on the sole of the foot. In 1896, the French neurologist Joseph Babinski noted that, when the foot's sole is stroked in a line from heel to toe, a healthy person's big toe will reflexively curl inwards. In patients with damage to their central nervous system, this reflex works in the opposite direction, causing the big toe to point upwards, and the other toes to splay outwards. An abnormal reflex like this — known as Babinski's Sign — can often prove one of the earliest signs of neurological damage.

# TOP 10 MOST COMMON NAMES IN THE USA

## BOYS

1. Jacob
2. Michael
3. Joshua
4. Matthew
5. Daniel
6. Christopher
7. Andrew
8. Ethan
9. Joseph
10. William

## GIRLS

1. Emily
2. Madison
3. Emma
4. Olivia
5. Hannah
6. Abigail
7. Isabella
8. Samantha
9. Elizabeth
10. Ashley

# SURNAMES

1. Smith
2. Johnson
3. Williams
4. Brown
5. Jones
6. Miller
7. Davis
8. Garcia
9. Rodriguez
10. Wilson

# WATER, WATER

## Rivers, lakes and seas

Lake Superior really is superior. It contains more water than all the other Great Lakes put together—enough to fill 4.5 billion Olympic-size swimming pools. Here are some more facts and figures about the rivers and lakes of the world.

The world's longest river, the Nile, is so vast that its drainage basin lies in 11 different countries.

Despite its name, the world's largest lake is the Caspian Sea in Western Asia. At 143,200 square miles, it is roughly the same size as Montana.

Scotland's Loch Ness is so deep that it contains more water than all the lakes in England and Wales combined.

At its widest point (Lake Winnibigoshish near in Minnesota); the Mississippi is 11 miles across. At its narrowest point (near Bena, Minnesota - Lake Itasca) it is just 30 ft. across.

The area of land drained by the river Amazon is equivalent to 1.3 billion football pitches.

In 2002, a Slovenian swimmer named Martin Strel swam the entire length of the Mississippi River. It took him 68 days. The project was called "eye to eye".

The drainage basin of the river Ganges is home to half a billion people, making it the most highly populated river in the world.

The largest lake in South America, Lake Titicaca, on the border between Peru and Bolivia, is also said to be the world's highest navigable lake. It lies 12,500 ft. above sea level.

Every second, the Mississippi River deposits 3,600,000 gallons of water into the Gulf of Mexico.

Europe's Danube flows through a record ten countries (Austria, Slovakia, Hungary, Croatia, Serbia, Romania, Bulgaria, Moldova, and Ukraine) and four capital cities (Vienna, Bratislava, Budapest, and Belgrade).

Lake Baikal in Siberia is the world's largest and deepest freshwater lake, containing around 22-23% of all the Earth's surface water—that's more than all five of the Great Lakes combined.

Lake Baikal is also claimed to be the world's oldest lake, but Lake Zaysan in eastern Kazakhstan may be even older. Some geologists claim that Zaysan was formed more than 70 million years ago, during the late Cretaceous period when dinosaurs would have still been walking around its shores.

It may only be 1% the size of Lake Superior, but O'Higgins Lake on the border of Chile and Argentina is the deepest lake in all of the Americas, dropping at one point to a depth of 2,743 ft. You could put the Chrysler Building and the Empire State Building in it, and still have room for the Space Needle!

# THE DISAPPEARING LAKE

Look at an old map of the world and to the east of the Caspian Sea, you'll see a smaller partner lake called the Aral Sea. Located on the border between Kazakhstan and Uzbekistan today, the Aral Sea was once the fourth-largest lake in the world, with a surface area of more than 26,000 square miles — twice the size of Maryland.

But from the mid-1900s onwards, the waters of the Aral Sea were diverted off to supply various irrigation projects in the Soviet Union in such a great quantity that, by the turn of the century, the lake had shrunk to just 10% of its original size. By 1997, the Aral Sea was reduced to four separate pools, the largest of which was barely 1,000 square miles in size. The remainder of the lake had dried up entirely, its seabed becoming what is now known as the Aralkum Desert.

There is hope for the future, however. After the Soviet Union dissolved and Kazakhstan declared its independence, the Kazakh government resolved to replenish the Aral Sea by building a series of dykes and dams directing water back into the Aral basin. These projects are still ongoing, but the early results are positive: in the five years from 2003–2008, waters in the northern section of what was once the Aral Sea rose by almost 40 ft., and the lake grew by more than 300 square miles.

*"A lake is the landscape's most beautiful and expressive feature. It is earth's eye; looking into which the beholder measures the depth of his own nature."*

**Henry David Thoreau**

# WARTIME:

## The story of the shortest war in history

Now part of the Republic of Tanzania (and not to mention a popular tourist destination), the tiny island paradise of Zanzibar off the east coast of Africa was for many years a British colonial protectorate, overseen by a local sultan loyal to British rule.

But on August 25, 1896, the reigning sultan, Hamad bin Thuwainian, suddenly died. His cousin, Khalid bin Barghash, quickly took to the throne and established a court for himself in the sultan's palace. Under ordinary circumstances, that would not have been a problem. But Khalid was not as loyal to the British forces as Sultan Hamad had been, and was much more critical of their rule in the region. Convention also dictated that the new sultan always be agreed to by the British authorities, and Sultan Khalid's accession did not meet with their approval. Instead, the British had their eyes on another more suitable successor, Hamoud bin Mohammed, so when Khalid suddenly stepped up and seized power, the British forces were compelled to act.

With their preferred ruler waiting in the wings, the British gave Sultan Khalid an ultimatum. On August 26, he was ordered to step down from power and hand over the throne to Hamoud or face the consequences. In response, Sultan Khalid doubled down. He assembled several hundred troops and supporters loyal to his rule and barricaded himself inside the sultan's palace. The British, sensing trouble, likewise assembled their forces: 1,000 British and Zanzibari troops were amassed, and a fleet of more than 100 British vessels arrived offshore. When the ultimatum expired at 9 a.m. the following day, the British declared war on Zanzibar.

Fighting broke out at 9:02 a.m. local time, when three Royal Navy ships—the HMS *Racoon*, HMS *Thrush*, and HM *Sparrow*—began bombarding the sultan's palace from offshore. It is said that one of the (if not *the*) very first direct hit of the battle destroyed one of the palace's main weapons, an enormous Arabian cannon, leaving those inside little chance of firing back. Out at sea, meanwhile, a former British vessel now in the service of the sultan, HMS *Glasgow*, joined the fray and began attacking another British ship, the HMS *George*. The *Glasgow* was quickly outmatched and sank in the shallow waters along with two local Zanzibari yachts. Their crews surrendered by hoisting British flags and were rescued from the ocean by British troops.

The bombardment of the palace continued until finally, at 9:46 a.m., Sultan Khalid's flag was shot down from the roof and a ceasefire was called. The battle—and ultimately the entire Anglo–Zanzibar War, as it became known; was now over. Although the precise timings of the events of the battle vary, the war is said to have lasted just 38 minutes. It is now considered the shortest battle, of the shortest war, in human history.

The British promptly installed Hamoud bin Mohammed as the rightful sultan, but to avoid any further uprisings, tightened their rule on the island. The protectorate endured for the next 67 years until Britain surrendered control of Zanzibar in 1963. The following year, it merged with mainland Tanganyika to form the United Republic of Tanzania, which became an independent country on April 26 1964.

As for Sultan Khalid, amidst all the fighting, he had escaped the palace through a back door along with a handful of his supporters and advisors and fled. Having initially sought asylum at the nearby German consulate, he was later smuggled back to the mainland but eventually apprehended, and was exiled by the British in 1916. He died in Kenya in 1927.

# THE 10 LARGEST COUNTRIES IN THE WORLD

| Country | Area in square miles (square km) |
|---|---|
| 1. Russia | 6,601,670 (17,098,246) |
| 2. Canada | 3,855,100 (9,984,670) |
| 3. China | 3,705,407 (9,596,961) |
| 4. United States | 3,677,649 (9,525,067) |
| 5. Brazil | 3,287,956 (8,515,767) |
| 6. Australia | 2,969,907 (7,692,024) |
| 7. India | 1,269,219 (3,287,263) |
| 8. Argentina | 1,073,500 (2,780,400) |
| 9. Kazakhstan | 1,052,100 (2,724,900) |
| 10. Algeria | 919,595 (2,381,741) |

Russia alone is large enough to cover roughly 11% of the entire land surface of the Earth. It is equivalent in size to all of South America.

Because Russia officially lays both in Europe and Asia, the only continent not represented in this Top 10 is Antarctica.

Because of its dual official languages, Canada is both the largest English-speaking and French-speaking country in the world. It is also the largest country in the Western Hemisphere.

Although it straddles the equator, the largest country in the Southern Hemisphere is Brazil. The largest country *entirely* in the Southern Hemisphere is Australia.

Australia is also the largest country in the world without any land borders with any others.

Argentina is the world's largest Spanish-speaking nation.

Kazakhstan is the world's largest landlocked nation.

The African republic of Sudan was once ranked tenth on this list (with an area of 967,500 square miles), but when South Sudan declared its independence and the country was partitioned in 2011, it fell to 15th place. Algeria took both its slot in the Top 10 and the title of the largest country in Africa.

# ALL ABOUT THE BENJAMIN

## Benjamin Franklin

Inventor. Scientist. Author. Philosopher. Polymath. Printer. Publisher. Diplomat. Founding Father. The life and achievements of Benjamin Franklin could fill an entire book, admittedly, but here are just a few interesting facts about him.

Franklin attended school for just two years. After that, his first job was working in the family business making soap and candles.

Franklin published his first essay when he was just 16, in his brother's newspaper, the *New England Courant*.

He used many pseudonyms for his writing over the years, including Silence Dogood, Harry Meanwell, Richard Saunders, Timothy Turnstone, Caelia Shortface, and Martha Careful.

Franklin's newspaper, the *Pennsylvania Gazette*, included a gossip column written by a 35-year-old columnist called Miss Alice Addertongue—but she was just another of Franklin's many pseudonyms.

Franklin retired when he was 42. Another of his newspapers, *Poor Richard's Almanack*, proved so successful that he was able

29

to retire in 1738 and dedicate the remainder of his life to other pursuits.

Franklin served as a delegate to both the Continental Congress and the Constitutional Convention, a diplomat and ambassador to both France and Sweden, the USA's first Postmaster general, and the president of the Supreme Executive Council of Pennsylvania. Despite that long history of public service, he never actively ran for elected office.

Although perhaps best known as the inventor of the lightning conductor, among Franklin's less well-known inventions were a type of flexible urinary catheter and a type of metal-lined fireplace known as a Franklin stove.

Franklin suggested that the English alphabet could be improved by ditching the letters C, J, Q, W, X, and Y, and adding six new phonetic symbols in their place.

He also invented bifocal spectacles—but despite popular opinion, he did not invent the rocking chair. Chairs fitted with rockers were already in use when Franklin was a child.

Although Franklin's countless inventions are best known for their contribution to science, he also contributed at least one to the world of music. While working in London, in May 1761, Franklin attended a performance by a musician named Edmund Delaval in Cambridge, England. Delavel was proficient in playing music on drinking glasses, which produced different tones by being filled with different quantities of water. Inspired by the concert, Franklin commissioned a local London glassblower to produce a series of 37 glass discs that could be fitted to a horizontal revolving spindle. Following Franklin's design, the different notes of the scale were color-coded: A was dark blue, B was purple, C red, D orange, E yellow, F green, G pale blue, and all the sharps and flats were painted white. Franklin called his device the "glass armonica" and his design received its world premiere in London in 1762.

*"[Benjamin Franklin] was the most accomplished American of his age and the most influential in inventing the type of society America would become."*

**Walter Isaacson**

# CUT!

## Stories of Hollywood casting changes

When it comes to making movies, producers and directors sometimes have more than one name in mind when it comes to making casting choices. And looking back at some of the names that could have appeared in some of Hollywood's most famous films, it's interesting to imagine how different these movies could have been!

### GONE WITH THE WIND (1939)

Margaret Mitchell's epic novel *Gone With The Wind* was published in 1936, won the Pulitzer Prize in 1937 and was adapted for cinema just two years after that. For the movie's romantic lead, Rhett Butler, Hollywood producer David O Selznick had his sights set on Clark Gable from the very start of production, and signed a lucrative deal with rival studio MGM to secure his involvement. However, for the role of Scarlett O'Hara, a total of 31 actresses were screen-tested, among them such Hollywood legends as Jean Arthur, Tallulah Bankhead, Susan Hayward, and Lana Turner. By the end of 1938, that list had been cut to just two: Paulette Goddard (known for her roles opposite her husband at the time, Charlie Chaplin) and British star Vivien Leigh. Goddard was seemingly Selznick's first choice: she was screen-tested in Technicolor before Leigh and Selznick later commented that Leigh had been the "dark horse" throughout the casting process. Nevertheless, concerns over 28-year-old Goddard's inexperience, her fiery relationship with the press, and her tempestuous private life (Chaplin was her second husband) meant that Leigh was eventually given the part.

## BEN-HUR (1959)

When it came to adapting the historical epic *Ben-Hur* for the big screen in the mid-1950s, the producers were faced with a monumental task: 50,000 performers appear on screen throughout the 212-minute movie, of whom more than 350 have speaking parts. When it came to the casting of the eponymous hero, meanwhile, the producers were spoilt for choice. Burt Lancaster was initially offered the role but turned it down, questioning the film's portrayal of Christian history. Marlon Brando, Kirk Douglas, Leslie Nielsen, and Rock Hudson were all also offered the part, but all turned it down — as too did Paul Newman (claiming that he didn't have the legs to wear a Roman tunic). Eventually, the role fell to Charlton Heston, who went on to win the Best Actor Academy Award for his performance.

## STAR WARS (1977)

Harrison Ford had already starred in George Lucas' *American Graffiti* when he was invited to merely act as a stand-in to help rehearse Han Solo's lines with other actors during pre-production for *Star Wars* in the mid-1970s. Both Lucas and the studio, 20th Century Fox, wanted a more established actor for

33

the role and had shortlisted the likes of Al Pacino, Christopher Walken, Jack Nicholson, Sylvester Stallone, Kurt Russell, and Nick Nolte for the part. Lucas was so impressed by Ford's impromptu performance in rehearsals, however, that he eventually offered him the role. He remains attached to the franchise to this day.

## DIE HARD (1988)

It might be many people's favorite holiday movie, but few people know that the classic thriller *Die Hard* was originally a book. Roderick Thorp's 1979 novel *Nothing Lasts Forever* was the basis for the film—and when it came to adapting the story for the big screen, that caused the production team and director John McTiernan a bit of a problem. Thorp's novel was the sequel to his 1966 book *The Detective*, which had been adapted for cinema in 1968 starring Frank Sinatra as the title character, Joe Leland. Leland was also the main character in *Nothing Lasts Forever*, and such was the way of Hollywood contracts at the time, the producers of *Die Hard* were legally obliged to offer the role to Sinatra before anyone else. Luckily for *Die Hard* fans everywhere, Sinatra—who was 73 years old at the time!—turned the role down, and it was offered to several of Hollywood's heavy hitters (including Arnold Schwarzenegger, Sylvester Stallone, Richard Gere, and Clint Eastwood) before Bruce Willis was finally cast. Producers later changed Joe Leland's name to John McClane, and the rest, as they say, is history.

## BATMAN (1989)

When Tim Burton cast *Beetlejuice* star Michael Keaton as Batman in his 1989 big-screen adaptation, some 50,000 comic book fans wrote to Warner Brothers to protest. Would any of the other big names attached to the project have received such a harsh reaction? Among those on the shortlist were Mel Gibson, Kevin Costner, Bill Murray, Pierce Brosnan, Charlie Sheen, Tom Selleck, Harrison Ford, Willem Defoe, and Dennis Quaid. Keaton's performance, however, eventually won the fans over—and he reprised the role two years later in *Batman Returns*.

## THE GODFATHER: PART III (1990)

Director Francis Ford Coppola famously cast his somewhat inexperienced daughter Sofia as Mary Corleone in the concluding part of his *Godfather* trilogy in 1990, and in doing so almost sunk the reputation of the entire series. She won an unprecedented two Golden Raspberry Awards for her performance, and even legendary Hollywood movie critic Leonard Maltin called her casting an "almost fatal flaw" in the *Godfather* series. Initially, Coppola had cast two-time Oscar-nominee Winona Ryder in the role of Mary and had auditioned several other Hollywood names (including Julia Roberts). But when Ryder was forced to pull out suffering from exhaustion, he was forced to cast Sofia at the last minute instead. Nevertheless, the final instalment in the Godfather trilogy eventually was nominated for seven Academy Awards, while Sofia Coppola later found fame behind the camera: in 2004, she became only the third woman in history to be nominated for the Oscar for Best Director—and won the award for Best

Original Screenplay—for her hugely acclaimed drama *Lost in Translation*.

## THE LORD OF THE RINGS TRILOGY (2001–3)

Sir Ian McKellen received his second Academy Award nomination for his role as Gandalf in Peter Jackson's epic *Lord of the Rings* series, but the role very nearly wasn't his. When production on the series' first began, producers initially looked to cast fellow Shakespearean actor Sir Nigel Hawthorne (known for his title role in *The Madness of King George*), but sadly he was too unwell to work at the time and passed away in 2001. Sam Neill, *Exorcist* star Max von Sydow, and Oscar winners Paul Scofield, Sir Sean Connery, and Christopher Plummer were all considered for the role too, as was Sir Christopher Lee (who was eventually cast as Gandalf's mentor, Saruman.) Also shortlisted was Sir Patrick Stewart, but when the producers were sent a videotape of him acting opposite his old friend Ian McKellen, they cast him instead.

# 10 MOST SUCCESSFUL OLYMPIANS OF ALL TIME

|  | Country | Discipline | Medals (Gold) |
|---|---|---|---|
| 1. Michael Phelps | USA | Swimming | 28 (23) |
| 2. Larisa Latynina | Soviet Union | Gymnastics | 18 (9) |
| 3. Marit Bjørgen | Norway | Cross-country skiing | 15 (8) |
| 4. Nikolai Andrianov | Soviet Union | Gymnastics | 15 (7) |
| 5. Ole Einar Bjørndalen | Norway | Biathlon | 13 (8) |
| 6. Boris Shakhlin | Soviet Union | Gymnastics | 13 (7) |
| 7. Edoardo Mangiarotti | Italy | Fencing | 13 (6) |
| 8. Takashi Ono | Japan | Gymnastics | 13 (5) |
| 9. Paavo Nurmi | Finland | Athletics | 12 (9) |
| 10. =Birgit Fischer | Germany | Canoeing | 12 (8) |
| =Bjørn Dæhlie | Norway | Cross-country skiing | 12 (8) |

Michael Phelps is not only the most decorated Olympian of all time, but he also holds the records for the total number of gold medals; the total number of gold medals from individual events; and the total number of medals from individual events. In fact, if team events (like relays) are excluded from this list, Phelps still comes out on top with a total of 16 medals, including 13 gold.

Phelps broke Soviet gymnast Larisa Latynina's longstanding record at the London Olympics in 2012 when he took his 19th gold medal in the men's 4 × 200 meter freestyle relay. Latynina's record had stood since 1964.

Phelps initially announced his retirement after the 2012 games but returned to the competition at the 2016 Rio Games to add a further five gold and another silver to his haul.

This list includes three Winter Olympians: skiers Marit Bjørgen and Bjørn Dæhlie, and biathlete Ole Einar Bjørndalen. All three represent Norway.

Marit Bjørgen's 15 medals make her the most decorated Winter Olympian in history.

The earliest name on this list is the Finnish middle- and long-distance runner Paavo Nurmi, who took home medals at the 1920 Games in Antwerp, the 1924 Paris Games, and the 1928 Games in Amsterdam.

Canoeist Birgit Fischer is the most successful Olympian to have represented more than one country. The gold medals she won in Moscow in 1980 and Seoul in 1988 were for East Germany, but after the fall of the Berlin Wall in 1989, the medals she won at the 1992 Barcelona Games, the 1996 Atlanta Games, the 2000

Sydney Games, and the 2004 Athens Games were all credited to the newly reunified Germany.

All the athletes on this list competed at multiple Games, but Fischer's total medal haul from six different years is more than any other.

The most successful Olympian to have only competed at a single Games is American shooter Willis Augustus Lee, who took home five gold, a silver, and a bronze all from the 1920 Games in Antwerp.

# POP QUIZ!

## AMERICANA

1.  What is the only U.S. state capital whose name begins with F?
2.  Who was the first Vice President to automatically assume the presidency after the death of a president?
3.  Which NFL team is based at Heinz Field stadium?
4.  At what Ivy League university was Facebook founded?
5.  The Aleutian Islands are part of what state?
6.  How was Harriet Lane, who served as First Lady to bachelor President James Buchanan, related to him?
7.  How many U.S. states have a shoreline on Hudson Bay?
8.  In what decade was the Academy of Motion Picture Arts and Sciences founded in Hollywood?
9.  In what state are Dell Computers based?
10. What is the most populous U.S. state capital?
11. What does the Q in NASDAQ stand for?
12. And what does the first A in NASA stand for?
13. In the 1960s, which Oscar-winning actress became the first star to be honored on the Hollywood Walk of Fame?
14. In what year of the 1990s was *Judge Judy* first broadcast?
15. In what city was Babe Ruth born?

16. Music stars Thelonious Monk, Nina Simone, James Taylor, and Tori Amos were all born in what state?

17. What was the first American city to host a Summer Olympic Games?

18. Alphabetically, which of America's National Parks comes last?

19. According to a 2017 survey, which U.S. state is the most religious—with 53% of its population attending weekly church services?

20. Which amendment to the U.S. Constitution prohibits cruel and unusual punishment?

# Answers

1.  Frankfort, Kentucky.
2.  John Tyler.
3.  Pittsburgh Steelers.
4.  Harvard.
5.  Alaska.
6.  Niece.
7.  None — Hudson Bay is entirely surrounded by Canada.
8.  1920s (1927).
9.  Texas.
10. Phoenix, Arizona.
11. Quotations.
12. Aeronautics.
13. Joanne Woodward.
14. 1996.
15. Baltimore.
16. North Carolina.
17. St Louis.
18. Zion.
19. Utah.
20. 8th.

# BEHIND THE WORDS

## Strange word histories and origins explained

In ancient times, the very basics of knowledge and learning were divided into a core set of subjects called the Seven Liberal Arts. The four scientific subjects of the seven were collectively known as the *Quadrivium*, literally the "four ways" of learning: astronomy, arithmetic, geometry, and music. The three linguistic subjects comprised the *Trivium*, or "three ways": grammar, logic, and rhetoric. Because this trio of were considered less intrinsic to our understanding of the world, the word *Trivium*—and later its plural, *trivia*—came to be used to refer to unnecessary or throwaway knowledge, precisely like the other surprising word origin stories in this chapter.

## DOGSBODY

As a word for a lowly servant or a menial worker, no one is entirely sure where the word *dogsbody* comes from. But the most likely theory is that it was originally a British naval term, and originally referred to a low-ranking crew member on a British vessel. Why the reference to a dog's body? It's thought the word might be inspired by the canine shape of the boiled bags of unappetizing meal or split peas that would be the usual sustenance of the ship's lowliest crew members.

## DIESEL

Diesel fuel, tanks, and engines all take their name from that of the 19th-century German scientist and engineer Rudolf Diesel, who invented a unique compression-ignition engine in 1892. Allegedly, Diesel himself was inspired to dedicate his life to improving transport after a particularly lengthy and grueling journey across Europe by train in his childhood. Tragically, his life was cut short in 1913 when he disappeared in unusual circumstances while on a ferry from Belgium to England. His body was never recovered from the North Sea. His innovations have since changed the world of transport forever—yet few people are aware of the extraordinary life of the man behind them!

## HANDICAP

There's an old myth that claims the word handicap derives from lame or injured soldiers who upon returned from overseas wars were unable to find employment and so turned to a life of begging on the streets—with their caps, quite literally, in their hands. In fact, the true story behind this word is even more peculiar. Originally, handicap was the name of a method of exchanging goods in a fair and proper manner. If two people were looking to trade, an impartial third party or umpire would assess the value of the items on offer.

If they were not of equivalent value, this umpire would then work out a cash value that the owner of the cheaper side of the bargain would have to add into the exchange to make it fair. The umpire would then hold out their cap, and if the traders agreed with their valuation, they would throw some loose change into the hat as a sign they were happy for the deal to go ahead. Any money thrown into the cap was the umpire's to keep, incentivizing them to make the deal a fair one.

It was this sense of assessing the relative value of things that eventually led to handicap horse races, in which better horses are encumbered with extra weights to keep the racing fair. Thus it was these lumbering, performance-reducing weights that eventually led to handicap being used to refer to anything that hinders someone or holds them back.

## GIRL

Oddly the word *girl* was originally gender-neutral (much like the word *child* is today) and could be equally applied to girls and boys. It is thought that it might derive from an Anglo-Saxon word for a child's swaddling cloth, but in truth, the very earliest origins are a mystery. After English picked up the male word *boy* from French, however, *girl* was forced to change its meaning and so came to be used exclusively for female children. It has remained in use in this way ever since.

## PIANO

Piano is short for *pianoforte*, which is itself built from the Italian words for "soft", *piano*, and "loud', *forte*. Pianos were so-called because their unique arrangement of hammers hitting strings to produce their sound made them one of the earliest keyboard instruments that allowed players to play at a range of different volumes. Earlier instruments, like harpsichords, had plucked the strings, and so were much more limited in the sounds they could produce.

## PANIC

We all know that panicky feeling we get in stressful situations, but few people know that the word we use to describe it is several thousand years old. Back in Ancient Greece, the goat-like god Pan (after whom the panpipes are also named) was associated with woodlands and forests. Pan was portrayed as a mischievous satyr and was believed to be responsible for all the eerie, disembodied noises that a lone person in the woods might be spooked by. That feeling of being unnerved or spooked ultimately came to be known as *panic* in honor of the ancient satyr once said to cause it.

## MEDIOCRE

The *medi*– at the start of mediocre is the same as in words like medium and mediate: it means "middle." The *–ocre*, however, comes from *okris*, an ancient Latin word for a rocky mountainside. The word *mediocre*, ultimately means "halfway up a mountain" — and it's in the sense of something being neither one thing nor the other, or merely halfway to completion or success, that the word eventually came to be used for anything only slightly impressive!

## SYLLABUS

Ironically for a word deeply associated with learning and education, the word syllabus owes its existence to a spelling error. *Sittybos* was an Ancient Greek word for a parchment scroll containing a table of contents, explaining the details and organization of other related documents. Latin scholars then picked up this Greek word in the 1400s, but they misread it and transformed its two neighboring T's into L's. They ultimately began using the newly invented word *syllabus* to describe a similar list of topics, and ultimately an itemized outline of a course or academic program.

## DENIM

The *denim* fabric used to make your favorite pair of jeans is named after the French city of Nîmes, where thick twilled fabrics like this (known as *serge*) were originally manufactured. The fabric we know today was originally the *serge de Nîmes*, and it's from those two French words running together that the word *denim* was born. The word *jeans* itself, incidentally, derives from the city of Genoa in nearby Italy.

## PARTRIDGE

Partridge birds are thought to take their name from an Ancient Greek word, *perdesthai*, literally meaning "to fart." When they take flight, the short and stocky birds make a loud drumming sound with their wings, which early hunters thought sounded a little bit like they were breaking wind!

# ELEMENTARY!

## Facts about Sherlock Holmes

Created by Scottish author Sir Arthur Conan Doyle, the impeccable detective Sherlock Holmes made his debut appearance in the tale *A Study in Scarlet* in 1887. He went on to become one of the most famous literary characters in history, portrayed on screen more than 250 times by 100 actors over 12 decades. Here are some more facts you might not have known about the world's most famous sleuth.

According to notes at the Museum of London, Sir Arthur Conan Doyle originally planned to call Sherlock "Sherrinford" but changed his mind before the publication of the first story in 1887. Dr. Watson, meanwhile, was originally named "Ormand Stacker."

The first time Doyle put pen to paper to write a Sherlock story, he wrote the line, "The terrified woman rushing up to the cabman."

It might be his catchphrase, but in none of Doyle's original stories does Sherlock ever say "Elementary, my dear Watson."

The first time "Elementary, my dear Watson" *did* appear in print was in 1915 — in a novel by one of Doyle's contemporaries, the novelist PG Wodehouse.

Famously, Sherlock's address is 221B Baker Street, London. The Sherlock Holmes Museum in London stands at #239 — but the City of Westminster officially permits the museum to use the #221B.

Sherlock is equally famous for wearing his characteristic deerstalker hat. But in none of the stories does Doyle explicitly say Sherlock's hat is a deerstalker.

Sherlock met Queen Victoria. In a story called *The Bruce-Partington Plans*, Sherlock is invited to Windsor to meet the Queen and is presented with an emerald tiepin.

Doyle dedicated the first collection of Sherlock stories to his old schoolteacher, Joseph Bell. Many people have since presumed Bell might have been the original inspiration for the character.

Sherlock's debut story, *A Study in Scarlet*, wasn't originally particularly popular. Turned down by numerous publishers, it was finally published in a magazine named *Beeton's Christmas Annual* in December 1887. Doyle was paid £25 for the rights by the magazine publishers.

Doyle wrote *A Study in Scarlet* in less than three weeks, alongside his work as a doctor in Portsmouth, a city on England's south coast.

The first print edition of *A Study in Scarlet* was illustrated by Doyle's father, Charles.

Doyle had to be convinced to write a second Sherlock Holmes story by a man named Joseph Stoddart, who edited another popular London periodical called *Lippincott's Monthly Magazine*. He met Doyle at a dinner party and offered to serialize a second Sherlock tale, effectively kick-starting Doyle's publishing career.

Sherlock has an older brother called Mycroft. Although some adaptations of Doyle's stories often make Mycroft's role a more significant one, he originally appeared in only two tales: *The Adventure of the Greek Interpreter* and *The Adventure of the Bruce-Partington Plans*.

The first time Sherlock Holmes appeared on camera was in 1900, in a short silent movie called *Sherlock Holmes Baffled*. Lasting just 30 seconds, the film was long assumed to be lost but was rediscovered in the Library of Congress in 1968.

*A Study in Scarlet* was adapted for cinema in 1914. Sherlock was portrayed by an accountant named James Bragington, hired not for his acting talent but his physical similarity to the character.

# FOOD FIGHT

## Timeline of food-based riots

Everyone has heard of the Boston Tea Party, but it's not the only food-related riot to have ever occurred. Here are some of the most significant and unusual that the history books have to offer.

### THE MOSCOW SALT RIOTS

The first half of the 17th century was a fraught and turbulent time in Tsarist Russia. Known as *Smuta* or "The Time of Troubles," the collapse of the great Rurik Dynasty—whose tsars had ruled over Russia for more than 750 years—sparked a violent succession crisis that crippled the country. The lack of power and stability in the highest levels of government led to widespread corruption, and although the situation improved with the establishment of the Romanov Dynasty in 1613, by then the Russian people were fed up. The implementation of a harsh salt tax in 1648 proved the final straw, and on June 2 a crowd of protestors stormed the Kremlin, demanding the tax be reversed and the corrupt governor of Moscow, Levontii Pleshcheyev, should step down. Pleshcheyev was eventually found, hauled from the Kremlin and killed, while the rioters went on to destroy more than 20,000 homes across the city.

51

## THE BOSTON BREAD RIOTS

In the early 1700s, the city of Boston was suffering from a critical lack of arable land on which to grow grain. What little grain was being grown locally, meanwhile, was often sold overseas; yielding great profits for the local traders but causing terrible food shortages in the city. Add to that the fact that trade disputes with England had closed many import and export routes and that many local businesses had started hoarding grain to artificially push up the price; before long, the local people were tired of the situation.

The problems sparked a series of three disturbances known as the Boston Bread Riots. In April 1710, a ship owned by a local grain trader named Andrew Belcher was attacked to stop its cargo of wheat from being shipped away and sold overseas. The following October, the situation was worsened by a huge fire that destroyed more than 100 homes and sparked a second riot. And in May 1713, the skyrocketing price of bread sparked a third riot involving some 200 people on Boston Common, which culminated in Belcher's ships and warehouses again being raided. The disturbances eventually forced a change in local legislation, prohibiting the export of locally-grown grain during local food shortages.

## THE DROGHEDA GRAIN RIOT

A century before the Irish Potato Famine of the mid-1840s, a series of unseasonably cold and dry winters in the 1730s led to an even more serious period of food shortages in 1740–41. Local supplies of milk, meat, grain, and potatoes were all affected by harsh late frosts and a prolonged drought and the dire situation was worsened by merchants selling what little produce was available to markets across the water in Scotland and England. Finally, in April 1740, a group of locals in Drogheda, north of Dublin, discovered a ship full of oatmeal bound for Scotland. They boarded the ship; broke its sails and rudder so that it could not leave port. The event sparked a short-lived disturbance in the city of Dublin, which saw shops raided and what little produce there was available inside sold off or given away to the crowds outside.

## THE NEW YORK FLOUR RIOT

Over the winter of 1836–37, the price of flour in the United States rose from around $7 per barrel to more than $12. The cost of rent and the prices of meat and coal all also increased as the questionable financial policies of President Jackson began to take effect. With the cost of staples like bread and flour now prohibitively high, by February 1837, the people of New York were ready for action. A meeting was called to protest the skyrocketing prices, and when a speaker happened to comment that a local tradesman named Eli Hart had stockpiled more than 50,000 barrels of flour in his storehouse, the assembled crowd of several thousand New Yorkers began to riot. Despite protestations from the Mayor, the crowd broke into Hart's warehouse (as well as those of other local traders) and looted much of his hoarded merchandise. Several dozen people were arrested in all—but not before hundreds of barrels of flour and wheat had been stolen, handed out, or destroyed.

## THE RICHMOND BREAD RIOT

During the American Civil War, food shortages sparked by disrupted trade routes and influxes of refugees in many towns and cities sparked numerous disturbances across the American South. On April 2, 1863, in Richmond, Virginia, the disturbances culminated in a protest organized by a local peddler named Mary Jackson. Jackson led a group of some 300 protestors—mostly women, and mostly in complete silence—through the streets of the city, where they proceeded to smash store windows and hold up shopkeepers while their stores were looted. Many thousands of dollars of produce were taken during the riot, but there was only one reported incident of bloodshed: one of the women either cut (or lost) some of her fingers reaching through a broken glass window. Jackson—who, according to legend, was arrested while brandishing a Bowie knife and shouting the protest's slogan …. "Bread or Blood!" was later tried for little more than a misdemeanor when it emerged that it could not be proved that she had stolen anything.

# THE BIG...

## Biggest things

The world's largest tree is a giant sequoia called General Sherman that stands in Sequoia National Park, in California. It is a full six feet taller—but oddly more than two feet narrower—than its nearest competition, another giant sequoia named General Grant. Here are some more facts and figures about some of the largest things in the world.

The Abraj Al Bait, a complex of skyscrapers in Mecca, Saudi Arabia, is home to the world's largest clock. Completed in 2012, each of the clock tower's four sides features a 141 ft. wide clock face. The clock was activated in August 2010 on the first day of Ramadan for a three-month trial.

Robert Waldow was the tallest man who ever lived. He stood 8 ft. 11.1 inches tall.

The world's largest orchestra—totaling 8,097 musicians—assembled in St Petersburg, Russia, on September 1, 2019.

The colossal squid is said to have the largest eyes of any living creature. Measuring 11 inches across, they're as large as a soccer ball.

The largest room in the White House is the East Room, a vast reception room used for banquets, balls, concerts, and conferences.

Of all major sports, polo requires the largest playing area: its field is 300 by 160 yards, equivalent in size to nine American football pitches.

Andean Condor is a new world vulture and the largest species of vulture family with biggest wingspans. The scavenger condor is one of the largest flying bird in the world, found in Argentina, Bolivia, Ecuador and Peru.

When the San Francisco 49ers beat the Denver Broncos to win Super Bowl XXIV in 1990, they won by the largest point's margin in the competition's history: 55 points to 10.

The largest stringed instrument that has ever been invented is called the *octobass*. Invented by a Parisian instrument-maker named Jean-Baptiste Vuillaume, the octobass is essentially a giant violin that stands 11 ft. 5 inches tall.

The world's largest sea is said to be the Mediterranean Sea. The Mediterranean Sea loses more water by evaporation than it is fed by the rivers draining into it. Thus, it has a steady inflow from the Atlantic. It has an area of 1,144,800 square miles and an average depth of 4,688 feet.

In 2012, a saltwater crocodile named Lolong was named the world's largest captive crocodile at a length of 20ft 3 inches. Lolong died in February 2013 in captivity.

The world's largest working telephone was unveiled at a festival in the Netherlands in 1988. Standing 8 ft. tall and weighing more than three tons, its 23 ft.-long handset needed to be lifted off with a crane to make a call.

The world's largest McDonald's restaurant opened in Orlando, Florida in 1970.

Rheasilvia is an impact crater on an asteroid named Vesta that orbits the sun between Jupiter and Mars. The center of the crater rises to an estimated peak of 82,000 ft. — making it the largest mountain in the solar system.

The world's largest cheesecake was baked in Stavropol, Russia, on September 23, 2017, to celebrate the city's 240th anniversary. It weighed 9,347 lb.

# ...AND THE SMALL

## Smallest things

At 6 ft. 4 inches, everyone knows Abraham Lincoln was the tallest president. But the shortest? That was James Madison, who stood just 5 ft., 4 inches tall. Here are a few more facts about many things that are the smallest of their type.

The world's smallest bird is the bee hummingbird. Weighing in at less than one-tenth of an ounce, they are typically just over two inches long.

The world's smallest ocean is the Arctic Ocean—though at over six million square miles in size, it's still one-and-a-half times the size of the United States!

The world's smallest inhabited island is Hub Island in the Thousand Island group lying between New York and Ontario. Home to one house, a single tree, a small beach, and some scrubland, it is somewhat appropriately also known as "Just Room Enough" Island.

At just 0.19 square miles (equivalent in size to 100 football fields), the Vatican City is the world's smallest country. It's so small that it is surrounded not just by Italy but by the city of Rome itself.

The world's smallest flag was a copy of the Canadian flag created at the Institute for Quantum Computing at the University of Waterloo in 2016. The flag was made by oxidizing a microscopic layer of silicon so that only parts of it turned red, recreating Canada's famous maple leaf on a piece of silicon 0.697 micrometers square—or just over one-billionth of a square inch.

The Carcross Desert in Yukon, Canada is a single square-mile of open dunes, flanked by snow-covered mountains and lush pine forests. Although its seasonal climate is too rainy to meet the official definition, the Carcross is nevertheless claimed to be the smallest desert in the world.

The smallest mammal in the world can be determined in two ways; either by the total weight or by the length. By total mass, the Etruscan shrew, a shrew species, is the smallest mammal, weighing at most two grams. The bumblebee bat is the smallest mammal by length and the size of the skull, measuring barely over an inch long.

England's smallest county, Rutland, is just 147.4 square miles in size—that's roughly one-tenth the size of Rhode Island. Its motto, *Multum in Parvo*, literally means "much in little."

The smallest skeletal muscle in the human body is called the stapedius. It controls the movement of the stapes, one of the three tiny bones inside the human ear, and is less than 0.05 inches long.

Found in the Andes area of South America, the Northern Púdu is the world's smallest deer. It stands barely 13-17 inches tall and weighs less than 13 lbs.

In 1939, the French actress Emile Marie Bouchand—better known by the stage name "Mademoiselle Polaire"— was measured to have the world's smallest waist: just 13 inches. The current record holder Ethel Granger has a waist of 13 inches.

The world's smallest hotel (the Eh'hausl hotel) is in Amberg, Germany. With only 570 square feet of floor space, it can only accommodate two guests at a time.

2,520 is the smallest number that can be equally divided by all the numbers from one to ten.

The Rotokas tribe of Papua New Guinea speak a language that uses the world's smallest alphabet. It uses just the 12 letters: A, E, G, I, K, O, P, R, S, T, U, and V.

Standing on a traffic island, Mill Ends Park on SW Front Avenue in Portland, Oregon, is officially the world's smallest park at just 452 square inches

Discovered in Indonesia in 2004, an extinct ancient hominid called *Homo floresiensis* is considered by anthropologists to be the human race's smallest ever relative. Individuals in this tiny race of early human beings that lived more than 13,000 years ago would have stood between 3 ft. 3 inches and 3 ft. 7 inches tall.

# OUT OF SIGHT

## Some famous disappearances

The fate of the 100 or so colonists at Roanoke, North Carolina, in 16th century is one of the strangest and longest-standing mysteries in history. Although it is widely believed the settlers simply assimilated into the communities of the native tribes living nearby, many other theories have been put forward over the years to explain their mysterious disappearance. Here are some of history's other most extraordinary unsolved disappearrances.

### THE PRINCES IN THE TOWER, 1483

The so-called Princes in the Tower are the young King Edward V of England (who was never crowned) and his brother Richard, the Duke of York. The pair were the only sons of King Edward IV and his queen, Elizabeth Woodville. When the king died on April 9, 1483, 12-year-old Edward, as the eldest brother, promptly succeeded to the throne. Edward's reign was short-lived, however, and he was never crowned. In June, he and his brother were declared illegitimate and deposed, with their uncle succeeding the throne in Edward's place as King Richard III. What happened to the two young princes is unclear, but it has long been believed that Richard, under the guise of protecting them, had them imprisoned in the Tower of London and ultimately murdered to ensure he could rule England with no threat to his power. How much Richard was indeed involved in their disappearance is the matter of much debate, but it is certainly true that there is no record of the brothers after the summer of 1483. Some human bones were discovered in the Tower about two centuries later, and Charles II ordered them to be interred in Westminster Abbey.

## THE CREW OF THE MARY CELESTE, 1872

The unsolved fate of the *Mary Celeste* is now so well known that its name has become synonymous with ghost ships, and indeed anywhere that is found to be deserted for equally mysterious reasons. The ship set sail from New York on November 5, 1872, bound for Italy. It was next seen floating off the coast of the Azores, an archipelago of Portuguese islands in the eastern Atlantic Ocean, still under full sail, with her hull still fully loaded, but with no sign of the crew. Nor was there any sign of a struggle, but maps and navigational equipment were missing, as was one of the lifeboats. The last entry in the captain's logbook had been made ten days earlier. What happened to the crew and the ship remain a complete mystery.

## AGATHA CHRISTIE, 1926

As the world-famous author of countless mystery stories including *Murder on the Orient Express* and *Death on the Nile*, it is somewhat ironic that Dame Agatha Christie was herself once the subject of a mystery. On the evening of December 3, 1926, Christie disappeared from her home in Sunningdale,

Berkshire, 20 miles west of London. The following morning her car was found parked above a quarry 15 miles south of their home, with little more than a change of clothes inside. There was no sign of Christie. The mysterious disappearance sparked a nationwide search, and the story even made the front cover of the *New York Times*. Some ten days later, Christie re-emerged: she had checked into a spa called the Swan Hydropathic Hotel in Harrogate, Yorkshire, 200 miles from London, under the name Mrs. Neele. She had no memory of how she had ended up there, but doctors later diagnosed a temporary form of amnesia sparked by stress and shock: Christie's husband had earlier demanded a divorce so that he could marry his lover, and on the evening before her disappearance, the couple had had a blazing argument at their home. The name of the husband's lover, tellingly, was Nancy Neele.

## JOSEPH FORCE CRATER, 1930

On August 4, 1930, New York Supreme Court judge Joseph Force Crater left a restaurant on West 45th Street in Manhattan, where he had been dining with a friend, walked out onto the street, and was never seen again. His disappearance proved such a scandal that the phrase "to do a Crater" entered 1930s slang as another way of saying that something or someone had gone AWOL. Quite what happened to Crater remains unsolved: known for his scandalous private life and his shady involvement in the corrupt Tammany Hall political machine, countless theories attempting to explain his disappearance have been put forward over the years, but none has ever been proved. Declared legally dead in 1939, the investigation into

Crater's disappearance was finally closed — still unsolved — some 40 years later, in 1979.

## AMELIA EARHART

On July 2, 1937, the airplane on which U.S. aviator Amelia Earhart and her navigator Frederick Noonan were traveling around the world disappeared in the southwest Pacific Ocean. This was the toughest and most grueling stretch of Earhart's journey: she had departed from Lae, in New Guinea, at midnight that night and had been due to arrive later that day at a tiny U.S.-controlled airbase on Howland Island, more than 2,500 miles away, to refuel. Having changed her altitude due to poor visibility, Earhart contacted a nearby U.S. vessel, the *Itasca*, to relay her amended height and to state that she was low on fuel. She was never heard from again. What happened to her and Noonan is unclear, but it is thought that perhaps due to a navigational error, the pair veered off course and, having wasted what little fuel they had left, Earhart was forced to ditch the aircraft. After a lengthy search, on July 18, 1937, the U.S. Navy concluded that the two must surely have died after crashing into the ocean. The tantalizing but equally unsolved discovery of human remains on Nikumaroro Island, a tiny islet in the Kiribati group, in 1940 has led to a longstanding theory that one or perhaps both of the pair survived the crash and lived for a time stranded on an isolated island, but alas this theory — along with many others — remains unconfirmed.

# CAPITAL IDEA

## World capital cities

Washington DC officially became the capital city of the United States on November 17, 1800, when the U.S. Senate convened at the Capitol for the very first time. Before then, Philadelphia had operated as the capital of America—and earlier still, the Continental Congress had convened in Philadelphia, Princeton, Annapolis, Trenton, and New York. Here are some more facts about the capital cities of the world.

La Paz, the administrative capital of Bolivia, is the world's highest capital city. It stands at an altitude of 11,975 ft. above sea level—although its sole airport, El Alto, stands even higher, at 13,325 ft.

Funafuti, the capital city of the tiny Pacific island nation of Tuvalu, is a name that means "banana woman."

Jakarta, the capital of Indonesia, is the fastest-sinking city in the world. Built on marshland and now home to ten million people, half the city is now below sea level.

In 2018, two British men named Adam Leyton and Chris Fletcher visited nine different capital cities—London, Paris, Brussels, Amsterdam, Berlin, Prague, Bratislava, Vienna, and

Budapest — in the space of 23 hours and 50 minutes. It remains the record for the most capitals visited in a single day.

The world's northernmost capital city is Reykjavík, Iceland.

The world's southernmost capital city is Wellington, New Zealand. (Although ironically it stands at the bottom of the North Island!)

Three countries have changed their capital city in the 21st-century: Naypyidaw took over from Rangoon as the capital of Myanmar in 2006, the tiny island nation of Palau moved its capital from Koror to Ngerulmud in 2006, and the east African republic of Burundi changed its capital from Bujumbura to Gitega in 2018.

The Vatican City is so small that it is technically its own capital.

The world's most dangerous capital city is said to be Caracas, Venezuela. For every 100,000 people living there, there are on average 75 homicides every year.

The world's safest capital city is Tokyo.

Thirty-four of the world's capitals are not their countries' largest city. Washington DC has only 1/12th the population of New York, while other capitals that are dwarfed by other cities include Canberra (which is 12 times smaller than Sydney, Australia), Ottawa (which is only a third of the size of Toronto, Canada), Wellington (which is six times smaller than Auckland, New Zealand), and Bern (which is a third of the size of Zürich, Switzerland).

The famous arches of the McDonald's "M" sign are white, not yellow, on the Champs-Élysées in Paris. The change was demanded by Parisian city planners, who disliked the bright yellow color of the normal logo.

The full Thai name for the city of Bangkok is *Krung Thep Mahanakhon Amon Rattanakosin Mahinthara Ayuthaya Mahadilok Phop Noppharat Ratchathani Burirom Udomratchaniwet Mahasathan Amon Piman Awatan Sathit Sakkathattiya Witsanukam Prasit.* With 168 letters, it is said to be the world's longest place name.

Manila is the Philippines is said to be the world's most densely-populated capital city, with an average of 119,600 people squeezed into every square mile.

Singapore is the world's most expensive capital city.

Just as the capital of Mexico is Mexico City, several other capital cities share their countries' names. The capital of Djibouti in Africa is Djibouti. The capital of Luxembourg is Luxembourg. Additionally the capitals of Panama, Guatemala, and Kuwait are Panama City, Guatemala City, and Kuwait City, respectively.

The world's coldest capital city is Ulaanbaatar in Mongolia, where temperatures seldom climb above -35°F over the winter.

In March 2019, 78-year-old Nursultan Nazarbayev suddenly stepped down as the president of Kazakhstan after 30 years in power. His successor, Kassym-Jomart Tokayev, was promptly sworn in in his place—but to the surprise of the Kazakh people used his maiden address to the nation to officially change the name of the country's capital city from Astana to Nursultan in Nazarbayev's honor. The change did not go down well, with online petitions promptly amassing thousands of names in opposition to the change. Nevertheless, the new name has remained in force ever since, with Nur-Sultan now widely recognized as the Kazakh capital's official name.

*"A walk about Paris will provide lessons in history, beauty, and in the point of life."*

**Thomas Jefferson**

# POP QUIZ!

## HISTORY

1. Built in Charlottesville, Virginia, in 1772, which great American statesman owned the plantation Monticello?
2. What date is written on the flag of Delaware?
3. Which Ancient Greek philosopher is known for living his life sitting in a barrel in the local marketplace?
4. What was the name of the international peace organization founded in Paris in the aftermath of World War I?
5. In what year of the 1980s did the UK and Argentina go to war in the Falkland Islands?
6. Which famous inventor was born in Milan, Ohio, on February 11, 1847?
7. Which of these famous heroes and villains was *not* born in the United States: Thomas Paine, Benedict Arnold, Martin Van Buren, or Lee Harvey Oswald?
8. The word *quisling* derives from the name of a Nazi collaborator who served in which country's government during World War II?
9. In what year did Elizabeth II become the queen of England?

10. Which Wild West outlaw and gunfighter's real name was Henry McCarty?

11. Which American religious leader founded Salt Lake City in 1847?

12. Which industrialist and philanthropist wrote a famous *Gospel of Wealth* in 1889, encouraging the rich to use their riches to improve society?

13. What was the first name of Mrs. O'Leary, the Irish immigrant whose cow is said to have started the Great Chicago Fire in 1871?

14. The ancient temple The Parthenon stands above which city?

15. Which British monarch was known as the Virgin Queen?

16. Which American industrialist is credited with inventing the assembly line?

17. Which of these ancient civilizations is said to have lived the furthest north: Inca, Maya, or Aztec?

18. Which famous English scientist, known for his work on gravity, served as a Member of the British Parliament for Cambridge University in the late 1600s?

19. In what century was Marco Polo born?

20. Which U.S. president won the Nobel Peace Prize in 1919?

# Answers

1.  Thomas Jefferson.
2.  December 7, 1787.
3.  Diogenes.
4.  The League of Nations.
5.  1982.
6.  Thomas Edison.
7.  Thomas Paine.
8.  Norway.
9.  1952.
10. Billy the Kid.
11. Brigham Young.
12. Andrew Carnegie.
13. Catherine.
14. Athens.
15. Elizabeth I.
16. Henry Ford.
17. Aztec.
18. Isaac Newton.
19. 13th century.
20. Woodrow Wilson.

# TOUCHING BASE

## Baseball

By the time Babe Ruth hit the first home run in the history of the All-Star Game at Comiskey Park in Chicago in 1933, he was already as one of baseball's greatest ever stars: Six years earlier, in 1927, he alone was responsible for hitting one in every seven of the home runs scored in his league that year. Here are some more facts about one of the USA's most popular sports.

On May 1, 1920, a game between the Boston Braves and the Brooklyn Dodgers lasted for 26 innings. It took three hours and 50 minutes to complete.

Fenway Park, Boston is Major League Baseball's oldest ballpark. It opened on April 20, 1912.

The world's largest baseball bat was made in 2000 by Fargo-Moorhead Red Hawks baseball club in Fargo, North Dakota, USA. It is 13 ft., 5 inches long and at its thickest is 40 inches in circumference.

The world's largest baseball went on display in Pittsburgh, Pennsylvania, in 2006. Signed by some of the game's best-known players, it measured 12 ft. in diameter.

When the Los Angeles Dodgers played the Boston Red Sox at the LA Memorial Coliseum in California March 29, 2008, more than 115,000 people attended — the biggest crowd ever assembled for a baseball game.

The world's oldest baseball diamond has been in use in Clinton, Massachusetts, since 1878.

To date, only 18 players have hit four home runs in a single regular-season game. The first was the Boston Beaneaters' Bobby Lowe in 1894.

On October 4, 2019, Matthew Graf of Louisville, Kentucky, threw a total of 2,633 baseball pitches in eight hours.

In 2008, Francisco Rodriguez made a record 62 saves in a single season, playing for the Los Angeles Angels.

The odds of being hit by a baseball while sitting in the stands has been calculated at 300,000 to 1.

In 2010, Aroldis Chapman of the Cincinnati Reds pitched a ball at 105.1 mph. That's faster than a cheetah's maximum running pace.

In 2002, Al Leiter of the New York Mets became the first pitcher in history to win against every other MLB team. To date, the feat has only been achieved by a total of 19 players.

In 2018, David Rush of Boise, Idaho, ran a 100 m sprint in a time of 14.28 seconds — while balancing a baseball bat on his fingertip.

# POLES APART

## Antarctica

Antarctica is not only the coldest place on Earth, but also the least populated, the least densely populated, the windiest, and technically the driest. Parts of Antarctica receive so little precipitation that they're technically a desert! Here are some more facts and figures about the southernmost place on earth.

Antarctica was completely ice-free until around 34 million years ago.

The driest part of the continent is Antarctica's aptly named Dry Valley. Covering around 1% of the entire continent, scientists believe these rocky gullies haven't seen rain or snow for two million years.

Three-quarters of all the Earth's fresh water is locked in Antarctica's ice.

The ice covering Antarctica is on average one mile thick— although at its thickest, the rocks below Antarctica are covered by more than three miles of ice.

Researchers working in Antarctica are so isolated and come from so many different backgrounds that they have been found to develop their accents of their own.

Because it sits on every line of latitude, technically Antarctica lies in every one of the world's time zones.

The South Pole is covered in ice and snow but very little of it falls from the sky there. In fact, on average Antarctica gets just 0.4 inches of precipitation per year.

The lowest temperature ever recorded on Earth was -128.6°F at the Vostok Station in Antarctica on July 21, 1983.

Antarctica's highest mountain, Vinson Massif, is 16,050 ft. tall.

The second tallest mountain in Antarctica, Mount Erebus, is also the southernmost active volcano in the world.

The highest temperature ever recorded in Antarctica was 69.3°F in February 2020.

The only resident population of Antarctica is scientists occupying the many permanent research stations that have been built there. Although the number of individuals living in Antarctica changes throughout the year, the population is roughly 5,000.

Blood Falls is the name of a bright red waterfall-like outflow seeping out of one of Antarctica's glaciers. Its blood-like appearance is caused by iron oxides—the same chemicals produced when metals rust.

It is estimated that more meteorites have been collected from Antarctica than any other continent, as the dry, cold climate stops the rocks from corroding.

Antarctica is the only continent in the world not home to spiders.

In 2013, rock band Metallica played a concert on an Argentinian Antarctic helipad—becoming the first music act in history to play a gig on every continent.

In 1898, a Belgian research ship called the *Belgica* became stranded in ice in the Bellingshausen Sea off the coast of Antarctica. To entertain themselves, the men on board organized a beauty contest of all the pictures of women they could find in a copy of a Paris newspaper that had been taken on board. The crew appointed a "Minister of the Land of Beautiful Women" who oversaw what they called a "Grand Concourse of Beautiful Women." Votes were cast on two bases: the photographs themselves (that saw "sporty girls" pitted against the likes of photos of "graceful dancers," "artistic poses," and "irreproachable character") and specific physical characteristics (including "sloping alabaster shoulders," "shapely hands," "luxuriant hair," and "flashing eyes"). It was intended that the women in the pictures be awarded prizes when the ship finally made it back to Europe, on the condition that they meet with the crew and posed for a photograph with them. Whether that ever happened or not is sadly unrecorded!

*"If Antarctica were music, it would be Mozart."*

**Andrew Denton**

# THE BIRD IS THE WORD

## Why are turkeys called turkeys?

Each Thanksgiving, Americans are estimated to eat some 45 million turkeys according to the U.S. Poultry and Egg Association—that means that, of all the turkeys eaten in the United States in an entire year, one-fifth are eaten in one weekend.

But have you ever stopped to think about why turkeys are called turkeys? After all, they don't come from Turkey—far from it, in fact, as the turkey we eat today is native to America. So where does the name come from and how did we get our geography so wrong?

To answer that, we need to go back in time—and back across the Atlantic Ocean—to Tudor England. The very first reference to a "turkey-cock" that we know about dates from the 1540s. Back then, the word was used to refer not to the large black-feathered fowl we know today, but to the African guinea fowl, a much smaller game bird native to the deserts and savannahs of central and southern Africa. These birds are believed to have become known as turkeys because it was via trade ports in the eastern Mediterranean Sea that they were imported across Europe: in fact, Turkey acted as a crossroads between African, Asian, and European markets, and the name *turkey* likely came to be attached to all manner of birds that passed through its ports.

When North American turkeys first began to arrive in Europe around a century later, the large, plump birds that roasted well and looked extraordinarily exotic compared to native European birds began to be referred to as "turkeys"—even though they were quite clearly imported into Europe from the west, not the east.

Nevertheless, the name soon stuck, and as American turkey became more popular and began to be traded and imported in ever larger numbers, it soon began to be used solely about them. We have called them turkeys ever since.

# MAKE IT SNAPPY

## Crocodiles and alligators

In 2016, a "psychic" saltwater crocodile named Burt correctly predicted the outcome of the Australian general election that year by snatching a picture of Prime Minister Malcolm Turnbull from a tank of fish guts, rather than his rival opposition leader Bill Shorten. Turnbull went on to secure a narrow electoral victory, with 54% of the votes. And even that story isn't the strangest fact about the world's biggest reptiles...

The very first crocodiles appeared around 250 million years ago—at the same time dinosaurs were still walking the Earth.

Crocodiles and alligators have no lips. They also cannot stick their tongues out.

Crocodiles are expert swimmers, but it was once thought that they tired easily and seldom swam long distances. Not so: a 2007 study of saltwater crocodiles found that some individuals cover as much as 30 km (18 miles) in a single day.

Even on dry land, crocodiles can easily run at speeds of 10-12 mph.

A group of crocodiles is called a bask.

The stomach acids of crocodiles are caustic enough to dissolve steel.

Some crocodiles have been found to swallow rocks to help them dive deeper underwater.

Crocodiles' faces are ten times more sensitive than your fingertips.

Crocodiles aren't all completely carnivorous: Around half of the world's species have been observed eating fruit.

The Florida Everglades is said to be the only place on earth where crocodiles and alligators can be found together.

Crocodiles have the strongest bite in the natural world. The largest saltwater crocodiles can slam their jaws shut with a force equivalent to 3,700 pounds per square inch — that's almost three times more powerful than a lion.

According to Lewis Carroll, "Nobody is despised who can manage a crocodile."

Crocodiles have superb homing instincts. In 2015, a massive 750 lb. saltwater crocodile in Queensland, Australia, was moved 250 miles from its home to avoid it being a threat to people living nearby. Three weeks later, it was spotted back in its usual home.

In 1919, a saltwater crocodile appeared on the island of Rotuma in Fiji. Crocodiles are not normally native to Fiji, and so it was calculated that the creature must have crossed the Pacific Ocean from the nearest known crocodile population — 600 miles away in Vanuatu.

In 2010, a plane crashed at Kinshasa Airport in the Democratic Republic of the Congo. In the aftermath of the disaster, it was found that the crash had been caused by many of the passengers and crew running to the front of the airplane to escape a crocodile that had been smuggled on board in a passenger's duffel bag. Shortly before landing, the crocodile got loose, and as the people on board fled from it in panic, the sudden transference of weight unbalanced the aircraft, causing it to crash. All but one of the 21 people on board was killed — but incredibly, the crocodile survived.

> *"If you wanted to dissuade a man from drinking his tenth whisky, you would slap him on the back and say, 'Be a man.' No one who wished to dissuade a crocodile from eating his tenth explorer would slap it on the back and say, 'Be a crocodile.'"*
>
> **GK Chesterton**

# POP QUIZ!

## MATH

1. What is the total of all the numbers from 1 to 10 inclusively?
2. What is 13 squared?
3. What is 2 × 4 × 6?
4. Expressed as a fraction, what is ½ × ¼?
5. What is 60% of 60?
6. What is the lowest three-digit prime number?
7. How many zeroes would one million millions have?
8. What is the sum of 111 + 222 + 333 =?
9. What is (5 × 50) + (6 × 60)?
10. What is 15/21 expressed in its simplest form?
11. Which of these numbers is not a factor of 3: 102, 123, 143, or 183?
12. What is the sum of the interior angles of a hexagon?
13. How many minutes are there between 2 p.m. and 8 a.m. the following day?
14. There are 10 red balls, 8 white balls, and 6 blue balls in a bag. What is the chance you will pick *either* a red or blue ball from the bag on your first attempt?
15. What is 7 × 8 × 9?

16. Subtract the square of 12 and the square root of 225 from 300. How much remains?
17. Which of these is the smallest: 8/15, 9/16, 10/17, or 11/18?
18. A numerical code lock comprising four independent wheels of numbers, 0–9, would have how many potential different combinations?
19. What is (99 × 3) + 3 = ?
20. If you were to write out all of the whole numbers from 1–100, how many times would you write a figure 7?

# Answers

1. 55.
2. 169.
3. 48.
4. 1/8.
5. 36.
6. 101.
7. Twelve (1,000,000,000,000).
8. 666.
9. 610.
10. 5/7.
11. 143.
12. 720°.
13. 1,080.
14. 2/3, or 66%.
15. 504.
16. 141.
17. 8/15.
18. 10,000 (because 0000 would also be permitted).
19. 300.
20. 20.

# HIGH RISERS

## Buildings that were once the world's tallest

New York's Empire State Building instantly became the tallest building in the world when it was completed in 1931. Standing 1,250 ft. tall, it was the world's first 100-story building and not only set the new world record but held the record as the world's tallest building for the next 41 years. The One World Trade Center that took its title in 1972—but since then, the title of world's tallest building has changed hands, and countries, several times. It looks set to change again in the future. But what about the past? Here are just some of the buildings that have held the title of world's tallest at some time in history.

### THE GREAT PYRAMID OF GIZA, EGYPT

The precise details regarding the pyramid's construction remain a mystery, as no written records have been found, but a number of estimates place its completion at sometime between 2560 B.C. and 2540 B.C. It is believed that it took two decades to complete the construction of Egypt's Great Pyramid at Giza, but when it was finally finished it stood around 481 ft. tall— instantly becoming the world's tallest building, by some margin, as early as 2,500 BCE. Erosion over the millennia that have followed has since taken around 25 ft. from that original height, but the Pyramid is believed to have held the title of the world's tallest building for more than 3,500 years.

## LINCOLN CATHEDRAL, UK

In 1311, construction was completed on a central third spire of Lincoln Cathedral in Lincolnshire in the east of England. The spire is believed to have stood at 525 ft., easily surpassing the Great Pyramid's height by more than 40 ft. Sadly, all three of Lincoln Cathedral's original trio of spires have since been lost: the taller central tower collapsed following a storm in 1548 and the remaining two smaller spires were taken down in 1807 when concerns were raised about their structural safety. Had the third spire remained intact, Lincoln Cathedral would have remained the world's tallest building until the completion of the Eiffel Tower in 1889.

## STRASBOURG CATHEDRAL, FRANCE

Nowadays the title of the world's tallest building seems to change hands every few years: When the Burj Khalifa in Dubai took the title from Taiwan's Taipei 101 in 2010, the Taipei had held the title for just six years. But Strasbourg Cathedral in eastern France held the title for an incredible 227 years. Standing at an impressive 466 ft., the cathedral was the world's tallest building from its completion in 1647 until 1874, when it was finally surpassed by St Nikolai's Church in Hamburg, Germany.

## THE WASHINGTON MONUMENT, USA

The first building in North America to hold the title of the world's tallest was a surprising one. On its completion in 1884, the 555 ft. Washington Monument became not only the world's tallest building, but the world's tallest wholly stone-built structure, and the world's tallest obelisk. The record didn't stay on this side of the Atlantic Ocean for long, however. The record returned to France just five years later with...

## THE EIFFEL TOWER

It was the Paris' Eiffel Tower that took the title from the Washington Monument, when it was constructed to celebrate the Paris World's Fair in 1889. Originally, the Tower was only intended to stand for the duration of the festival, but it proved so popular with guests (and proved so useful as a telegraph tower during World War I) that its original 20-year permit has been extended indefinitely. At 1,063 ft., it comfortably held the title of the world's tallest building for 41 years—until it was beaten by the Chrysler Building in 1930.

# THE BIG DEAL

## Stories about card games

The earliest paper playing cards were originally Chinese. Produced sometime around the 7th century CE, they were typically organized into animal-based suits, not the spades, hearts, clubs, and diamonds we know today. Here are some more facts about figures about playing cards and card games.

There are 52 cards in a standard deck — and a total of 52 letters in the words ace, king, queen, jack, ten, nine, eight, seven, six, five, four, three, and two.

Not all decks have that many cards, however. A piquet deck only has 32: the seven, eight, nine, ten, jack, queen, king, and ace of all four suits.

The card game euchre is played with an even smaller deck: with all the cards from two to eight removed, a euchre deck only has 24 cards in total.

Two euchre decks make a pinochle deck: a total of 48 cards.

Some card games enforce a so-called "British Rule," that stipulates that the queen outranks the king whenever the British monarch is female.

Traditionally, a deck of bridge cards is slightly narrower than a standard poker deck. Poker cards are 2 1/2 inches wide, while bridge cards are 2 1/4 inches. Both are 3 1/2 inches in length.

The fastest time a full deck of cards has ever been dealt is 16.92 seconds.

The fastest time a shuffled deck of cards has been put back in order is 36.16 seconds.

In Thailand, it has been illegal since 1953 to own more than 120 individual playing cards.

In 18th-century England, a deck of cards was nicknamed "a history of the four kings."

Each of the face cards in a deck is popularly said to represent someone from history. The four kings are said to represent David, Charlemagne, Julius Caesar, and Alexander the Great.

The chance of being dealt a royal flush in a game of poker is roughly 650,000 to 1.

In 2019, a Buddhist Canadian man named Scott Wellenbach won $671,000 in a poker tournament—and promptly gave it all away to charity.

A hand containing the ace and eight of spades and clubs is known as a dead man's hand—it was reportedly the hand held by Wild Bill Hickok when he was shot and killed in 1876.

Mathematically, the total number of different ways that a pack of 52 cards can be shuffled is 52!, or 52 factorial. As a figure, that is equal to approximately $8 \times 10^{67}$, or 80 centillion—although the precise figure is actually this:

80,658,175,170,943,878,571,660,636,856,403,766,975,
289,505,440,883,277,824,000,000,000,000

To get your head around how vast a number that is, think about this: The Grand Canyon has been estimated to have a volume of roughly 146 trillion square feet. It would take 416 billion trillion grains of sand to fill it to the top. If you were to put one grain of sand in the Grand Canyon every second for each possible combination of a shuffled deck of cards, it would take you 13.2 quadrillion years to complete the task. Put another way, even if you started your job at the very dawn of the universe — which scientists estimated was around 13.8 billion years ago — today you would still only be around 1/95,000th of the way through completing the task, or around 0.001% of the way to completing it.

# POP QUIZ

## SCIENCE

1. What is the most abundant gas in the Earth's atmosphere?
2. The Fahrenheit temperature scale and the centigrade system are numerically equal at what temperature?
3. What is the common name for the bone that is anatomically known as the sternum?
4. Ornithology is the study and science of what creatures?
5. What is a material that will not carry an electrical charge called?
6. Pd is the chemical symbol for what metallic element?
7. What was the number of the *Apollo* lunar mission that took the first humans to the moon?
8. How many planets in our solar system have no moons?
9. What was the name of the first supersonic passenger aircraft?
10. Scurvy is caused by a deficiency of what vitamin?
11. In Einstein's famous equation $e = mc^2$, what does the C represent?
12. What are the filaments of incandescent light bulbs typically made from?
13. Housed in West Orange, New Jersey, what was Thomas Edison's Black Maria the earliest example of?

14. What is the rapid cooling of molten glass to form solid sheets or shapes of glass called?
15. What fraction of a second is called a nanosecond?
16. What is the scientific study of trees called?
17. What blood type is considered universal, meaning it can be donated to anyone regardless of their own blood type?
18. What is the longest bone in the human body?
19. The syrinx is the part of a bird's body that allows it to do what: sing, lay eggs, fly, or navigate?
20. In what century was the first patent issued in the United States?

# Answers

1. Nitrogen.
2. –40°.
3. Breastbone.
4. Birds.
5. Insulator.
6. Palladium.
7. *Apollo 11.*
8. Two.
9. Concorde.
10. Vitamin C.
11. The speed of light.
12. Tungsten.
13. Movie production studio.
14. Quenching.
15. One billionth.
16. Dendrology.
17. O negative.
18. Femur (thighbone).
19. Sing.
20. 18th century.

# THE 10 MOST-WATCHED TV MOMENTS IN U.S. HISTORY

|  | Broadcast | Audience |
|---|---|---|
| 1. | The Apollo 11 Moon Landings (1969) | ~150,000,000 |
| 2. | Super Bowl XLIX (2015) | 114,400,000 |
| 3. | Super Bowl XLVIII (2014) | 112,200,000 |
| 4. | Super Bowl 50 (2016) | 111,900,000 |
| 5. | Super Bowl LI (2017) | 111,300,000 |
| 6. | Super Bowl XLVI (2012) | |
| 7. | Super Bowl XLV (2011) | 111,000,000 |
| 8. | President Nixon's resignation speech (1974) | ~110,000,000 |
| 9. | Super Bowl XLVII (2013) | 108,7000,000 |
| 10. | Super Bowl XLIV (2010) | 106,500,000 |

## THE 10 MOST-WATCHED TV FINALES IN U.S. HISTORY

|  | Broadcast | Audience |
|---|---|---|
| 1. | *M\*A\*S\*H* (1983), *Goodbye, Farewell & Amen* | 105,000,00 |
| 2. | *Cheers* (1993), *One For the Road* | 84,400,000 |
| 3. | *The Fugitive* (1967) *The Judgment: Part 2* | 78,000,000 |
| 4. | *Seinfeld* (1998) *The Finale* | 76,300,000 |

5.  *Friends* (2004) *The Last One*                            52,500,000

6.  *Magnum, P.I.* (1988) *Resolutions*                         50,700,000

7.  *Tonight Show Starring Johnny Carson* (1992)   50,000,000

8.  *The Cosby Show* (1992) *And So We Commence*  44,000,000

9.  *All In The Family* (1979) *Too Good Edith*           40,200,000

10. *Family Ties* (1989) *Alex Doesn't Live Here*       36,300,000
    *Anymore*

# ONE MISSING

## Artists who have never had a #1 single

As of 2020, all of the bands and artists listed here have never had a #1 single on the Billboard Hot 100 chart. Some have come close — some, several times — but all of them have missed out.

### AC/DC

Rock legends AC/DC have charted on the Hot 100 a total of seven times but have never even broken into the top 20. They reached their peak in 1991 when *Money Talks* reached #23. Among their other famous tracks, *Highway To Hell* peaked at #47, *Back In Black* reached #37, and *You Shook Me All Night Long* reached #35.

### BACKSTREET BOYS

They've sold 100 million records worldwide and have had three #1 albums, but the Backstreet Boys have never had a #1 single on the Hot 100. The closest they've come was *Quit Playing Games (With My Heart)*, which peaked at #2 in 1997.

## BOB DYLAN

*Like A Rolling Stone* (1965) and *Rainy Day Women #12 & #35* (1966) both peaked at #2, kept from the top spot by The Beatles' *Help!* and the Mammas and the Pappas' *Monday, Monday*, respectively.

## BRUCE SPRINGSTEEN

The Boss has had nine #1 albums but has never had a #1 single. *Dancing in the Dark* hit #2 in 1984—but was kept from the top spot by Duran Duran's *The Reflex*.

## CREEDENCE CLEARWATER REVIVAL

*Proud Mary, Bad Moon Rising, Lookin' Out My Back Door/Long As I Can See The Light*, and *Green River* all peaked at #2.

## DON HENLEY

As one of the Eagles, Don Henley scored five Billboard #1s, including *Hotel California* in 1977. As a solo artist, he has reached the Top 10 on five separate occasions, and spent six weeks at #2 as a guest artist on Patty Smyth's *Sometimes Love Just Ain't Enough* in 1992.

## EN VOGUE

One of the most successful female groups of the 1990s, En Vogue, has missed out on a #1 single on three separate occasions. *Hold On* was held off the top spot by Glenn Medeiros' *She Ain't Worth It* in 1990. Two years later, *My Lovin' (You're Never Gonna Get It)* was kept off the top by Kris Kross' *Jump*. And *Don't Let Go (Love)* was kept at bay by Toni

Braxton's *Un-Break My Heart* in 1997. Their other biggest hit, 1994's *Whatta Man*, peaked at #3.

## GREEN DAY

When *Boulevard of Broken Dreams* peaked at #2 in 2005, Green Day scored their highest-charting Hot 100 single to date.

## JAMES BROWN

The Godfather of Soul's songs have charted more than 90 times, but the closest he has ever come to the top was with *I Got You (I Feel Good)*, which peaked at #3 in 1965.

## JIMI HENDRIX

*All Along The Watchtower* peaked at #20 in 1968.

## JOURNEY

Did you think *Don't Stop Believin'* was a #1 single? No, it peaked at #9 in 1981. Journey's highest-charting single, *Open Arms*, reached #2 in 1982 but was kept off the top spot by The J Geils Band's *Centerfold*.

## THE KINKS

The Kinks have scored three Billboard Top 10 singles but have never broken the Top 5.

## KISS

Kiss has charted on the Hot 100 a total of 24 times, but only two of their tracks have ever broken the Top 10. *Beth/Detroit*

*Rock City* reached #7 in 1976 and, 14 years later, *Forever* reached #8 in 1990.

## LED ZEPPELIN

*Whole Lotta Love* reached #4 in 1974, but Led Zeppelin never charted any higher.

## LYNYRYD SKYNYRD

Add this to your list of songs you thought reached #1: *Sweet Home Alabama* only reached #8 in 1974.

## MARTHA REEVES & THE VANDELLAS

They scored a total of six Top 10 hits, but never secured the top spot: *Dancing in the Street* peaked at #2 in 1964.

## METALLICA

Metallica has scored six consecutive #1 albums but have never had a #1 single. They've only reached the Top 10 once, when *Until It Sleeps* peaked at #10 in 1996.

## NIRVANA

It's one of the most iconic songs of the 90s but *Smells Like Teen Spirit* peaked at #6 in 1991.

## NO DOUBT

If you thought *Don't Speak* was a Billboard #1, think again. It held the #1 position on the airplay chart for 16 weeks in 1996 (a record at the time), but because no commercial version of the single was released, it was not eligible to chart on the Hot 100. No Doubt's highest chart position came in 2002, when *Underneath It All* reached #3.

## ONE DIRECTION

They reached #2 in 2013 with *Best Song Ever*, but this British five piece has never scored a #1.

## RED HOT CHILI PEPPERS

They've reached the Top 10 three times, and *Under The Bridge* peaked at #2 in 1992 — but the Chili Peppers have never scored a #1 single.

## R.E.M.

*Losing My Religion* reached #4, *Stand* reached #6, *The One I Love* peaked at #9, and *Shiny Happy People* reached #10. As for *Everybody Hurts*? It never charted any higher than #29.

## SHERYL CROW

Incredibly, Sheryl Crow has never had a #1 album or single on the Billboard chart. *All I Wanna Do* peaked at #2 in 1994, and while eight of her albums have charted inside the Top 10, none has ever hit the top spot.

## TALKING HEADS

*Burning Down The House* peaked at #9 in 1983.

## TORI AMOS

Trailblazing singer-songwriter Tori Amos has charted six times on the Billboard Hot 100 to date but has only ever broken into the Top 50 once: *Spark* peaked at #49 in 1998.

## THE WHO

Incredibly, The Who only reached the Billboard Top 10 once, when *I Can See For Miles* reached #9 in 1967.

# BRAZIL NUTTY

## The country of Brazil

Brazil is a country of superlatives. It's the largest country in South America, the largest country in the southern hemisphere, and the fifth-largest country in the world. It's also the world's sixth-most populous country, with a population of over 210 million people, and the second-most forest-covered country after Russia. Here are some more fascinating facts about this remarkable country.

Brazil shares a land border with all but two of the other countries in South America. Only Chile and Ecuador miss out.

They may be 5,000 miles apart, but technically France's longest land border is shared with Brazil via French Guiana, a vast overseas department of France lying on the north coast of South America.

The world's largest coastal lagoon is the 174-mile long Lagoa dos Patos in southern Brazil.

Half the world's orange juice comes from Brazil.

Brazil covers almost 48% of the entire continent of South America.

Brazil is so vast that the country's most easterly point is closer to Africa than it is to its own largest city, São Paulo.

Brazil is home to more than 16,000 species that are not found anywhere else on Earth, making it perhaps the most biodiverse country on the planet.

Brazil is home to the world's largest Portuguese-speaking population and the world's largest Catholic population. Brazil is the only Portuguese-speaking nation in the Americas.

Brazil is home to 22 UNESCO World Heritage Sites—that's two more than Canada and only two behind the USA.

The largest book ever printed was a 6 ft., 7-inch tall edition of *The Little Prince* made for the Rio Book Fair in 2007.

At 135 ft., *Kilimanjaro* at the Aldeia das ÁguasPark Resort in Barra do Pirai, Brazil, is the world's tallest waterslide.

In 2018, a Brazilian man named Walter Orthmann set the world record for the longest employment at a single company. Orthmann started his job as a shipping assistant at Industria Reneaux in Santa Catarina, Brazil, in 1938 at the age of just 15. Eight decades later, he was still employed there at the age of 96—and still walked to his office every morning!

Ilha da Queimada Grande, a tiny 106-acre island off the Brazilian coast, is nicknamed Snake Island because it has on average one snake for every square meter of terrain. There are so many snakes on the island that people are forbidden to visit it without permission from the Brazilian Navy.

The name of Rio de Janeiro—the former capital city of Brazil and one of the largest cities in the world—literally means "river of January".

In 2019, 120 dogs attended a screening of the animated movie *The Secret Life of Pets 2* in São Paulo. In 2005, the mayor of Biritiba Mirim, a town in southern Brazil, proposed introducing a ban on death (but with no penalty) because the local cemetery had reached its capacity.

The Brazilians are known for their lover of soccer and their national team certainly doesn't let them down. Brazil has won the FIFA World Cup a record five times, in 1958, 1962, 1970, 1994, and 2002. They are also the only team to have won the World Cup on four different continents and are the only national team in the world to have qualified for every FIFA World Cup since the competition began in the 1930s. Their playing record is just as remarkable: As at 2020, Brazil have won two-thirds of all the World Cup matches they have played in and from 1993–96 the national team went undefeated in a record 35 consecutive matches. The worst score line that Brazil has ever recorded in a World Cup tournament was in 2014, when Germany unexpectedly defeated them by 7–1. It was the first time the team had lost by more than six goals in 94 years and the first time the team had ever trailed by more than four goals during any World Cup match in the entire history of the tournament.

*"They have a joy for life in Brazil unlike any country I've ever seen."*

**Morena Baccarin**

# THE 20 LARGEST OBJECTS
# IN THE SOLAR SYSTEM

|  | Object | Mean diameter *(miles)* |
|---|---|---|
| 1. The Sun | Star | 865,373 |
| 2. Jupiter | Planet | 88,846 |
| 3. Saturn | Planet | 74,9 |
| 4. Uranus | Planet | 31,763 |
| 5. Neptune | Planet | 30,779 |
| 6. Earth | Home planet | 7,926 |
| 7. Venus | Planet | 7,521 |
| 8. Mars | Planet | 4,222 |
| 9. Ganymede | Moon of Jupiter | 3,27 |
| 10. Titan | Moon of Saturn | 3,2 |
| 11. Mercury | Planet | 3,031 |
| 12. Callisto | Moon of Jupiter | 2,996 |
| 13. Io | Moon of Jupiter | 2,264 |
| 14. The Moon | Earth's moon | 2,159 |
| 15. Europa | Moon of Jupiter | 1,94 |
| 16. Triton | Moon of Neptune | 1,68 |

| | | |
|---|---|---|
| 17. Pluto | Dwarf planet | 1473 |
| 18. Eris | Dwarf planet | 1,445 |
| 19. Titania | Moon of Uranus | 979 |
| 20. Haumea | Possible dwarf planet | 888 |

All eight of the planets in our solar system make this list, but Mercury, the smallest, is outranked by two planetary satellites, Ganymede and Titan.

If Saturn's rings were included in its diameter, it would jump to second place on the list: At their widest, the rings are about 180,000 miles across.

Ranking this list by mass rather than diameter would change things around too. Neptune is smaller but denser than Uranus, and so would rank fourth by mass alone.

Mercury would jump to ninth place above Ganymede and Titan; Pluto would drop below Eris into 18th place and Titania would fall into 20th place, behind Haumea.

Twelve of the entries here have been discovered in modern times. The earliest are the four so-called Galilean moons of Jupiter—Ganymede, Callisto, Io, and Europa—that were discovered by Galileo in 1610.

Only two have been discovered in the 21st century: Eris in 2003 and Haumeau in 2004.

# SPACED OUT

## The planets

When it was discovered in 2003, the dwarf planet Eris gave astronomers a bit of a headache. At almost 1,500 miles in diameter, it was larger than Pluto, but its orbit was misshapen and unclear, so astronomers weren't keen to class it as a planet in its own right. Eventually, an entirely new category of astronomical object—the "dwarf planet"—was created to account for unusual outliers like Eris. Unfortunately for Pluto, that decision led to its category being changed too and it was officially downgraded in 2006. Here are some more facts and figures about the objects in our solar system.

The Sun is large enough to contain every other object in the solar system inside of it.

The giant red spot on the surface of Jupiter is an immense storm that has been circling the planet for 400 years.

Venus takes the equivalent of 243 Earth days to complete one full planetary rotation. Because it only takes 224 days to orbit the Sun, a year on Venus is shorter than a day.

The distance from a central star (like the Sun) at which an orbiting planet (like the Earth) can support surface water and an atmosphere is known as the "Goldilocks Zone" because the orbital characteristics need to be just right.

In 1984, Thomas O. Paine, the third Administrator of NASA, designed a flag for Mars.

Neptune emits more light than it receives from the Sun.

Although Mercury is closest to the sun, the atmosphere of Venus is so hostile that it is actually the hottest planet.

Scientists believe that, four billion years ago, Mars had an ocean covering just under one-fifth of its entire surface.

The clouds on Venus are made of sulfuric acid.

Jupiter's magnetic field is so bizarre that the planet has two south poles.

The same chemical that makes blood red is what makes Mars look red.

Titan, the largest moon of Saturn, is the only moon in the solar system to have an atmosphere of its own.

In 2004, a "triple eclipse" of Jupiter occurred when three of its orbiting moons— Io, Ganymede, and Callisto—passed between it and the Sun and all simultaneously cast their shadows onto its surface.

Seven of the 79 natural satellites of Jupiter discovered so far have not been seen since their discovery and are currently considered to be lost.

Saturn's rings are around 50,000 miles wide—but only 30 ft. thick.

Neptune was discovered in 1846. To our knowledge, it did not complete its first orbit of the sun until 2011.

It rains diamonds on Neptune.

Io, one of the largest moons of Jupiter, is home to 400 active volcanoes, making it the most geologically active body in the solar system.

The surface of Titan is covered in lakes of liquid methane.

Saturn is nine times larger than the Earth—but only 1/8th its density.

Rhea, one of the largest of Saturn's moons, has a bright white impact crater on its surface nicknamed The Splat.

Winds on Neptune blow at more than 1,100mph—meaning the wind on Neptune is faster than the speed of sound.

*"The sun, with all those planets revolving around it and dependent on it, can still ripen a bunch of grapes as if it had nothing else in the universe to do."*

**Galileo Galilei**

# AND THE WINNER IS...

**How the Oscars have changed since their very first year**

Nowadays, the annual Academy Awards ceremony is one of the entertainment industries most prestigious and hotly-anticipated nights, attended by some of the world's most famous names, and watched globally by an eager audience of a billion people. But the very first Academy Awards ceremony — held quite late in the year, on May 16, 1929 — was an entirely different affair.

Hosted by the actor, movie director, and producer Douglas Fairbanks — the then President of the Academy of Motion Picture Arts and Sciences — the very first ceremony was a private dinner, held at the Hollywood Roosevelt Hotel in Los Angeles, California. It was a curiously small occasion compared to the grand program we know today. No live broadcast was made publicly available (that would begin with a live radio broadcast the following year) and only 270 people were in attendance, each of whom had bought a ticket for the princely sum of $5.

Awards were handed out in just 12 categories, with a great many differences from those in place today. There were, for instance, two separate directors' awards — one for comedy and one for drama. Likewise, the equivalent of the Best Picture award was also divided in two back in 1929: one award went to what was termed the year's most "Outstanding Picture" (won by the World War I epic *Wings*) and another went to what was described as the "Best Unique and Artistic Picture" (awarded to the romantic drama *Sunrise*). Both these very first Best Picture winners were, of course, silent pictures.

Relatively speaking, so few films were made in the early days of the Academy Awards that the awards ceremony focused on all those Hollywood movies that had been released over the previous two years, not one. So the very first Best Picture honoree, *Wings*, had been released some 21 months before it won the award, in August 1927!

The awards for Best Actor and Best Actress were likewise awarded not to an actor's single performance but for several impressive roles across the previous year. As these were the days of silent pictures, an Oscar was also awarded for Best Title Writing—the text that appears on screen in place of dialog. This category was discontinued the very next year, so the inaugural winner of the Title Writing Academy Award, silent movie impresario Joseph W. Farnham, remains the only person in history to have won it. (Incidentally, one of Farnham's fellow nominees in the Title Writing category, the silent-era screenwriter Gerald Duffy, had passed away the previous year—making him the very first posthumous Oscar nominee.) Awards for Best Original Story, Best Written Adaptation, Art Direction, Cinematography, and Engineering Effects completed the roster of categories and have remained on the Academy's list in one form or another ever since.

But of all the curiosities behind the very first Academy Awards, perhaps the most glaring compared to today's Oscars is that the winners in each category were not a mystery on the night. Everyone who won an award at the 1929 ceremony had been told of their victory a whole three months earlier and the ceremony was merely a celebratory event at which they could all collect their prizes. Perhaps for that reason, the entire prize-giving section of the night only lasted a mere 15 minutes—somewhat different from the four-hour television marathon we're used to today!

# A PHAROAH'LD TIME

## Ancient Egypt

Reserved exclusively for the leaders of Ancient Egypt, the word *pharaoh* means "great house." In that sense, it probably originally referred to the grand palaces in which the pharaohs of the ancient world resided. Here are some facts and figures about these ancient god-kings and their equally ancient kingdom.

The great pyramids of Ancient Egypt are all tombs, built to house the bodies and belongings of great Egyptian figures.

Most pyramids were fitted with a tomb chapel that allowed grieving families to sit with, visit, and even eat and drink beside their relatives long after they had passed.

To date, more than 130 pyramids have been discovered across Egypt.

The Pyramid of Khufu at Giza is the largest Egyptian pyramid.

The average Egyptian mummy was wrapped in almost a mile of bandages.

Both male and female pharaohs ruled over Egypt—and both were expected to wear makeup. The characteristic black shapes around the pharaohs' eyes were thought to enhance their appearance and reduce glare from the African sun.

Ramses II, better known as Ramses the Great, ruled Egypt for almost 67 years and lived to be over 90 years old.

Pepy II became pharaoh when he was just 6 years old—but ruled Egypt for the next 94 years. His throne name, Neferkare (Nefer-ka-Re), means "Beautiful is the Ka of Re ".

Not all pharaohs were quite so long-lived: Tutankhamen was just 19 when he died.

Quite what happened to King Tut is a mystery, but examinations of his remains have led to the suggestion that he may have been killed by a hippopotamus or a crocodile while on a royal hunting expedition. In 2014, producers of a BBC television documentary postulated that Tut died in chariot crash that broke his legs and pelvis, and resulted in an infection and perhaps death by blood poisoning. Supporters of this theory note that Tut was depicted riding on chariots and also suffered from a deformed left foot, making it possible that he fell and broke his leg.

The Egyptians did not ride camels. Domesticated camels did not arrive in Egypt until long into the days of the Egyptian Empire, at the very end of the dynastic age.

Egyptian scribes rarely wrote in hieroglyphics. These beautiful symbols were special. They were used only for carved inscriptions and formal documents. Day-to-day Egyptian language was written using a simpler shorthand system called "hieratic" text.

The Egyptians were known for playing a board game called "dogs and jackals."

The Pyramids were not built by slaves but by paid laborers and masons. It's also likely that farmers and farmhands were involved in their construction during the periods of flooding when they could not work on their lands.

The Egyptians' fondness for a diet rich in beer, wine, and honey led to health problems. Medical examinations of some mummies have shown that some rulers likely suffered from diabetes.

Hatshepsut, the first female pharaoh, wore a fake beard. The pharaohs were considered the living embodiments of the gods and because the great god Osiris was portrayed with a long black braided beard, she too was expected to wear one.

The queen we know only as Cleopatra today was Cleopatra VII — the seventh Egyptian ruler with that name.

Also, Cleopatra wasn't Egyptian. A member of the Ptolemaic dynasty of rulers, like much of her family, she was culturally more closely aligned with Ancient Macedonia than Egypt and was descended from one of the lieutenants of Alexander the Great.

There are rumors that Cleopatra was not as beautiful as history would have us believe. The Greek poet and historian Plutarch said that her beauty actually lay in her voice and demeanor, not in her appearance.

*"The Pyramids are perfect. But you can't
put the Pyramids in the middle of Manhattan.
In the desert, the combination of light and form makes it perfect."*

**I. M. Pei**

# POWERHOUSE

## The White House

Construction of the White House began three years into George Washington's first presidential term, in 1792. Work to complete the house took over eight years, however, this meant that the first president to occupy the house was his successor, President Adams. The famous West Wing was added in 1901 by President Roosevelt and it was left to his successor, President Taft, to add the Oval Office in 1909. Here are some more facts and figures about the most powerful house in the world.

The White House was designed by an Irish architect named James Hoban, who based it on Leinster House, the former palace of the Dukes of Leinster, in Dublin, Ireland.

No one knows for sure where the sandstone the house is built from comes from. The most likely theory is that it was brought in from a quarry in Virginia, but popular history claims it was shipped from Pučišća quarry in modern-day Croatia — where the sandstone used to build the palaces of Ancient Rome was sourced.

Before moving into the White House, John Adams lived in the President's House, a grand mansion in Philadelphia. It was later converted into a hotel but is no longer standing today.

The name "White House" was first used in 1811, but it only became the official name under President Roosevelt in 1901. Before then, the house was officially known as the "President's Palace," the "Presidential Mansion," or simply the "President's House."

John Adams moved in on Saturday, November 1, 1800. The following day, he wrote his wife Abigail to say, "I pray Heaven to bestow the best of blessings on this House, and all that shall hereafter inhabit it."

James Madison spent only five of his eight years as President in the White House. After the Burning of Washington by British troops in 1814, he was forced to see out his term first from Octagon House, a grand red-brick townhouse in the Foggy Bottom neighborhood of Washington, D.C., and then from the city's Seven Buildings complex on Pennsylvania Avenue while the White House was rebuilt.

In 1867, Nathaniel Michler proposed abandoning the use of the White House as a residence and designed a new estate at Meridian Hill, Washington. The plan was rejected by Congress.

When Chester A Arthur took office in 1891, he found the White House too crowded and sold 20 wagonloads of furniture and artifacts at a public auction.

Thanks to modifications made in the early 1900s due to President Roosevelt's ill health, the White House is often claimed to be one of the first major wheelchair-accessible buildings in the world.

President Jimmy Carter added solar-powered water-heating panels to the White House. They were removed by Ronald

Reagan but reinstalled by George W. Bush in 2003. President Obama added more in 2013.

There are 35 bathrooms in the White House.

There are six different stories in the entire building, connected by eight staircases—but only three elevators.

Residents of the White House can choose from one of 28 fireplaces to warm themselves by!

It takes 570 gallons of paint to coat the outside of the White House.

To keep presidents entertained, the White House has a jogging track, movie theater, bowling lane, tennis court, and swimming pool.

The grounds of the White House cover 18 acres.

Today, tours of the White House are—understandably—formal, ticketed affairs that have to be booked and scheduled in advance. But before the early 1900s, the doors of the White House were all but permanently open to the public, which led to all kinds of run-ins between the president and his public over the house's long history.

President Lincoln was famously dogged by crowds of job-hunters and armchair politicians on many days during his presidency, including local Washington eccentric "General" Daniel Pratt, who left the president a lengthy screed of suggestions before being escorted from the premises. Of all the public incidents in the House's long history, however, perhaps one of the strangest took place after the inauguration of President Jackson in 1829. After he was sworn in, Jackson opened the White House doors to a crowd of some 20,000 revelers — who promptly became so drunk that the President was compelled to retire to a local hotel for the evening.

The only way the crowd could be convinced to disperse back out onto the White House grounds was by luring them outside with enormous washtubs full of orange juice mixed with whisky.

*"The White House is the finest prison in the world."*

**Harry S. Truman**

# TOP MARX

## Groucho Marx's quotes

The third eldest of the legendary Marx Brothers, Julius Henry "Groucho" Marx, was born on October 2, 1890, in New York City. In a career spanning six decades, he established himself as a comedian, actor, writer, producer, and raconteur on screen, stage, radio, and TV. He remains one of America's best-loved entertainers, known for his almost impossibly quick wit and his superb one-liners. Here are some of Groucho's best lines:

*"I refuse to join any club that would have me as a member."*

*"A hospital bed is a parked taxi with the meter running."*

*"Outside of a dog, a book is a man's best friend. Inside of a dog it's too dark to read."*

*"Alimony is like buying hay for a dead horse."*

*"I find television very educating. Every time somebody turns on the set, I go into the other room and read a book."*

*"A man is only as old as the woman he feels."*

*"I never forget a face, but in your case I'll be glad to make an exception."*

*"Behind every successful man is a woman, behind her is his wife."*

"I must confess, I was born at a very early age."

"One morning I shot an elephant in my pajamas. How he got into my pajamas I'll never know."

"Go, and never darken my towels again."

"The secret of life is honesty and fair dealing. If you can fake that, you've got it made."

"My favorite poem is the one that starts 'Thirty days hath September,' because it actually tells you something."

"There's only one way to find out if a man is honest: Ask him. If he says yes, you know he's a crook."

"I have a mind to join a club and beat you over the head with it."

"From the moment I picked your book up until I laid it down, I was convulsed with laughter. Someday I intend reading it."

"Next time I see you, remind me not to talk to you."

"I need a doctor immediately. Ring the nearest golf course."

"A black cat crossing your path signifies that the animal is going somewhere."

"Why, a four-year-old child could understand this report! Run out and find me a four-year-old child – I can't make head nor tail out of it."

"Quote me as saying I was misquoted."

# THERE'S NO PLACE LIKE HOME

## The Wizard of OZ

Based on L. Frank Baum's *The Wonderful Wizard of Oz*, the iconic 1939 film *The Wizard of Oz* has gone on to become one of the most popular and influential Hollywood films of all time. Here are some little-known facts and figures about one of the silver screen's longest enduring classics.

*The Wizard of Oz* premiered at a cinema in Green Bay, Wisconsin, on August 10, 1939. The Hollywood premiere did not take place until five days later.

It was first shown on television in 1956.

*The Wizard of Oz* was nominated for five Academy Awards, winning for Best Score and Original Song. Judy Garland was also presented with a special "Juvenile Award" for her performance.

Dorothy's slippers were originally made of silver in the book. It was movie screenwriter Noel Langley that changed them to ruby for the film version so that they would show up more on the big screen in glorious Technicolor.

Ray Bolger, who played the Scarecrow, was initially cast as the Tin Man.

Buddy Ebsen (who went on to star in *The Beverly Hillbillies* in the 1960s) was the original Tin Man, but he was forced to leave the production after he had an allergic reaction to the aluminum-based makeup powder the role required. He was replaced by Jack Haley—and the aluminum powder was replaced with a less irritating paste!

Margaret Hamilton, who starred as the Wicked Witch of the West, suffered burns to her face and hand during a scene using pyrotechnics. The sparks ignited the bright green powder used in her makeup.

Wanting a simple, lyrical tune for the movie's main music number, composer Harold Arlen based part of the melody of *Somewhere Over The Rainbow* on a children's piano exercise.

*Somewhere Over The Rainbow* was the last song written for the film.

*Somewhere Over The Rainbow* was at one point cut from the movie because MGM chief executive Louis B Mayer thought it "slowed down the picture." Luckily, it was later reinstated!

The tornado was made from 35 feet of muslin cloth suspended from the ceiling.

The 'oil' used to lubricate the Tin Man's joints on screen is chocolate syrup.

The fake snow that falls on Dorothy as she sleeps in a field of flowers was partly made of asbestos.

A song called *The Jitterbug* was cut from the theatrical release of the film and its footage was later lost. Only a recording of the song and some old home-movie footage of rehearsals for its dance number have survived.

The movie was originally a bomb for MGM, who recorded losses of over $1 million in 1939. Later re-releases and a lucrative television broadcast deal with CBS allowed it to finally turn a profit a decade later.

Although *The Wizard of Oz* is credited to the legendary Hollywood director Victor Fleming, Fleming left the production in February 1939 to take over the reins on the troubleshot set of *Gone With The Wind*. Fleming's long-time friend King Vidor took over as the director of *Oz*, directing the tornado scene, many of the other opening sepia-and-white scenes, and Dorothy's famous performance of *Somewhere Over The Rainbow*. On its release, Vidor opted to keep his name from the film's credits and, out of respect to his friend, largely kept his contribution to the movie quiet until after Fleming's death in 1949. Vidor and Fleming were actually just two of the four directors whose names were attached to the film, however. The project was initially given to Richard Thorpe, but his approach to the film's appearance proved too saccharine for the producers and he was fired after less than two weeks' work. Next, it was given to George Cukor, but he too was promptly removed from the set and made to work on *Gone With The Wind* before Fleming took over.

*"We still watch [The Wizard of Oz] … because its underlying story penetrates straight to the deepest insecurities of childhood, stirs them, and then reassures them."*

**Roger Ebert**

# OOPS!

## Stories of accidental inventions

In 1943, engineer Richard T. James accidentally knocked a spring from a high shelf in his office at a Philadelphia shipyard. He watched as it neatly uncoiled itself and stepped its way down from the shelf onto a table, and then onto the floor. Two years later, the very first Slinky toys went on sale in America! Here are some more astounding stories behind some of the world's most unexpected inventions.

### PENICILLIN

The Scottish physician Sir Alexander Fleming famously discovered the antibacterial agent penicillin growing in a moldy Petri dish on a windowsill in his London laboratory in 1928. Although the use of penicillin-based molds in medicine has been known about for centuries, Fleming's discovery and research brought their use right up to date and made the widespread application of such antibacterial agents possible. He was jointly awarded the Nobel Prize for Medicine for his work in 1945. Some other medicines that are said to have been discovered by accident include insulin, Viagra, and quinine.

## SILLY PUTTY

When rubber was rationed in the United States as a result of World War II, scientists and engineers across the country sought to produce a simple synthetic replacement. One decidedly unexpected result of these early experiments was Silly Putty, a stretchy, bouncy, rubber-like substance made from a mixture of boric acid and silicone oil. There are at least two rival claims to its invention, one from chemist Earl L. Warrick and another from Scottish-born engineer James Wright.

## CORN FLAKES

Dr. John Harvey Kellogg and his younger brother Will Keith Kellogg were both working at Battle Creek Sanitarium, Michigan, in 1894 when a mash of dough made from boiled and pulped wheat was accidentally left out, uncovered, on a worktop in the hospital kitchens. Having dried out almost completely overnight, when the dough came to be rolled out, rather than squishing down under the weight of the roller, it splintered into hundreds of individual flakes. Curious to know what these small flakes tasted like, the brothers baked them in the oven. The result: Corn Flakes cereal.

## POST-IT NOTES

In 1968, Texas-born chemist Spencer Silver was seeking to produce a super-strong adhesive in the research laboratories of the Minnesota Mining & Manufacturing Company (now 3M) when he accidentally invented the exact opposite: a super-weak adhesive, capable of sticking things together only temporarily. His discovery sat unused in the 3M company records until 1973 when one of Silver's colleagues realized his glue could be used commercially to produce temporary bookmarks and paper tags. Originally marketed as the "Press-N-Peel," the product became a hit when rebranded as the Post-It Note in 1980.

## PLAY-DOH

In the mid-1950s, the Kroger supermarket company approached Kutol Products, a Cincinnati-based soap manufacturer, to produce a pliable and slightly tacky substance that could be used to remove coal dust from wallpaper. The project fell to Kutol chemist Noah Vicker, who produced just such a substance—apparently from an otherwise closely guarded recipe of flour, water, starch, and borax—in 1955. But as cleaner natural gas domestic heating systems began to replace coal fires, the market for a wallpaper cleaning putty vanished, and Kutol was forced to rethink their product to save the company from bankruptcy. Remarketed as a child's toy, Play-Doh has since become a childhood staple.

## VULCANIZED RUBBER

According to legend, American chemist and engineer Charles Goodyear threw a lump of sulfur-coated rubber onto a stove in a fit of frustration—and found that, rather than melt, it developed a toughened, blackened, charred outer shell. Later experiments improved this chance discovery, and the use of both intense heat and sulfur compounds to strengthen and treat rubber became the hallmark of Goodyear's newly-named "vulcanized" rubber.

*"To invent, you need a good imagination
and a pile of junk."*

**Thomas Edison**

# ALL THAT JAZZ

## Jazz Music

No one knows for sure why jazz music is so-called. One theory is that it comes from *jasm*, a term for vim and vitality first used in the mid-19th century, which by the early 1900s had perhaps morphed into a word for a new, energetic, rule-breaking style of music and dance. Whatever the origins of its name, the music we call jazz is one of the most important inventive styles of music in the world—and here are some facts and figures all about it.

According to the *Oxford English Dictionary*, the earliest written record of the word *jazz* dates from 1912.

One of the jazz world's most recorded musicians is the American bassist Ron Carter. He has more than 2,221 recording credits to his name.

The first jazz records were recorded and released by the Original Dixieland Jazz Band in New York in 1917. Their first recording was *Indiana and the Dark Town Strutters' Ball*—but it was released several weeks after their first album release, *The O.D.J.B.'s Livery Stable Blues*, which was released on March 7, 1917.

The world's largest jazz festival is held in Montreal, Canada. Nearly 1,913,868 jazz fans attended the festival on its 25th anniversary in 2004.

Listening to jazz music has been found to reduce anxiety as much as a massage.

The first jazz Grammy Awards went to Ella Fitzgerald and Count Basie. They won the Best Jazz Performance awards — for a solo and group performer, respectively — in 1959.

On July 17, 2010, jazz saxophonist Kenny G scored his 14th #1 recording on the U.S. Contemporary Jazz album chart. He holds the record for the most jazz #1s in music history.

According to a study by John Hopkins University, when jazz musicians improvise, their brains turn off the part of the brain that controls self-censorship, inhibition, and introspection.

According to a glossary of slang terms Benny Goodman published in 1937, an *alligator* is a jazz fan that doesn't play a musical instrument themselves.

The most expensive record ever to chart in the United States was the complete CD set of *Miles Davis at Montreux*, which entered the U.S. Jazz charts in November 2002. Each copy had a cover price of $250!

When jazz star Ray Charles' album *Genius Loves Company* was nominated for Album of the Year at the 2004 Grammy Awards, it made history: Charles' last nomination in the same category was *Genius + Soul = Jazz* in 1961, and that 43-year gap between his two Album of the Year nominations is the longest in music history.

When Quincy Jones was nominated for the Best Jazz Performance by a Large Group Grammy Award in 1961 for his album *The Great Wide World of Quincy Jones*, it was the first of many. As of 2020, Jones has been nominated for 80 Grammy Awards—more than any performer in history.

According to Wolfram researcher and mathematician Jon McLoone, *jazz* is the hardest dictionary word to guess in a game of Hangman.

French jazz pianist Michel Petrucciani is said to have been the shortest professional pianist in history. On his death in 1999, he stood just 3 ft. tall.

According to the *Guinness Book of Records*, jazz standard *Summertime* by George Gershwin (taken from his acclaimed opera *Porgy and Bess*) is credited with being the most recorded song in music history with more than 67,000 known versions recorded since it was written in 1934.

# GOING SWIMMINGLY

## Swimmers and swimming

American swimmer Michael Phelps is the most-decorated Olympian in sporting history. Before his retirement at the end of the Rio Games in 2016, he had amassed a total of 28 medals — of which an astonishing 23 were gold. Here are some more facts and figures about swimming, swimmers, and swimming record-holders.

Until the 1940s, male competitive swimmers were expected to wear full-body swimming suits.

Understandably, a swimming "marathon" is not quite as long as a running marathon: It is swum over a distance of 10,000 meters.

At the 1908 Olympic Games in London, a 100 meter-long swimming lane was built inside the running track of the athletics arena.

The 1908 Olympics were also the first at which the swimming event took place in an actual swimming pool: Before then, Olympic swimming had taken place in the Mediterranean Sea (1896 and 1906), the river Seine (1900), and in a lake (1904).

The world's deepest diving pool is in Montegrotto Terme, Italy. Plunging to more than 137 ft., it contains more than 1.1

million gallons of water. Opening in late 2019-2020, Deepspot, which is currently under construction near Warsaw, will be the deepest diving pool in the world. With a depth of 45 meters and containing 8,000 cubic meters of water, 27 times as much as in an ordinary 25-meter swimming pool, the Deepspot pool will be as deep as a fifteen-story building.

In 2019, Iranian swimmer Elham Sadat Asghari swam 5,488 m (3.4 miles) — all while handcuffed.

The very first modern Olympic Games — held in Athens, Greece, in 1896 — featured a swimming event that was open only to members of the Greek Navy.

In a 2012 survey by the Water Quality & Health Council, one-fifth of all American adults admitted that they urinated in swimming pools.

Synchronized swimming has only been an Olympic event since 1984 — and has only been a team event since 1996. Before then it was only open to solo and duet competitors.

Many Olympic swimmers wear two swimming caps: an inner cap made of slip-proof fabric and a smoother outer cap to reduce drag in the water.

The best hand position for swimming at speed is said to be to split the fingers slightly apart, allowing a swimmer to "rake" the water as they go.

When he took the plunge in an ice-covered Andean lake 20,899 ft. above sea level in 2019, Australian adventurer Daniel Bull set the record for the highest-altitude swim in human history.

The word SWIMS still reads "SWIMS" even when turned upside down.

The Lexis Hibiscus Port Dickson resort in Malaysia has 643 individual swimming pools, more than anywhere else on Earth.

In 2006, Croatian swimmer Veljko Rogošić spent 50 hours and ten minutes swimming the 140 miles across the Adriatic Sea from Grado to Riccione, off the Italian coast. It was the longest distance ever swum without flippers in the open ocean.

In 2019, a team of 100 swimmers set the record for the 100 x 50m swimming relay: together, they took just over 43 minutes and 32 seconds to swim a combined 5,000 meters!

*"Only the man who is swimming against
the stream knows the strength of it."*

**Woodrow Wilson**

# BRAND NEW:

## The invention of Coca-Cola

The world's first batch of *Coca-Cola* was concocted by the Atlanta chemist John Stith Pemberton in May 1886.

Born in Knoxville, Georgia, in 1831, Pemberton was a Civil War veteran who had been badly injured during the conflict and had struggled with morphine addiction in the later years of his recovery. Looking to create a refreshing, flavorful tonic that could help him overcome his reliance on more harmful painkillers, Pemberton cooked up a rich caramel-colored syrup from a generous mixture of botanical extracts—including extracts from the nut-like fruit of the Indian "kola" tree.

Happy with his recipe, Pemberton took the very first batch of his tonic just a few doors down from his home to a local chemist's store, Jacob's Pharmacy, in the center of Atlanta. There he mixed it with carbonated water to create a longer, fresher drink and began trialing his invention on the pharmacy's customers. They all soon approved of his recipe—and the very first draughts of Pemberton's new fizzy tonic were sold for the princely sum of five cents a glass.

It was the accountant of Jacob's Pharmacy, Frank Robinson, who first named Pemberton's invention *Coca-Cola*, coining the snappy-sounding name based on the kola extract it contained, while simultaneously presuming that the name's two alliterative letter Cs would look impressive on the drink's branding. Indeed, it was Robinson too who invented the drink's now world-famous handwritten-style logo. Sometime later, *Coca-Cola* made its very first appearance in print in an Atlanta newspaper ad that called it a "delicious and refreshing beverage."

The following year, Pemberton registered his "Coca-Cola Syrup and Extract" label as a copyright with the U.S. Patent Office. But in 1888, he took desperately ill and was forced to sell many of his holdings to fellow an Atlanta pharmacist named Asa Griggs Candler. Pemberton made $1,750 from the sale — a lot of money at the time certainly (equivalent to more than $50,000 today), but a sum that still seems somewhat puny given how immense the *Coca-Cola* brand is today.

Alas, however, Pemberton would not live to see his invention become the world leader it now is. His sudden sickness was soon afterward diagnosed as cancer, and he passed away just a few months after selling his final stake in the *Coca-Cola* brand in 1888. The recipe was now Asa Candler's to do with what he wished, and under his guidance and funding, production of *Coca-Cola* was ramped up to an industrial scale. Soon there were manufacturing plants and sales were points all across the city, and within just a few short years, there would be *Coca-Cola* plants not just across the United States, but Canada and Central America too.

By the turn of the century, *Coca-Cola* was already well on its way to becoming one of the worlds' most successful and recognizable drinks brands.

# POP QUIZ!

## SPORT

1. Which Major League Baseball team is subject to the so-called "Curse of the Bambino"?
2. How many competitions comprise a tennis Grand Slam?
3. ...And of all the contests in a Grand Slam, which one is held earliest in the year?
4. In what decade were the Winter Olympics first held?
5. Telemark, Nordic, Alpine, and Super-G are all forms of what sport?
6. In baseball, what might be characterized as a 12–6, an 11–5, or a 2–8?
7. In yards, how long is a cricket pitch? 18, 22, 28, or 36?
8. Why was there no baseball World Series competition in 1994?
9. What name is given to the winter sport combining cross-country skiing and rifle shooting?
10. FINA is the international governing body of what sport?
11. What nationality is tennis star Stan Wawrinka?
12. In American football, what name is given to a long pass, typically thrown in the dying seconds of a game, despite there being little chance of its success?

13. Which of these sports is played on ice: bandy, shinty, korfball, or handball?

14. The Nürburgring is a Formula One racing circuit in what European country?

15. Which country's national soccer team won two out of the first four FIFA World Cup competitions in 1930 and 1950—but have since never finished any better than fourth place?

16. In volleyball, what is the maximum number of times a team is permitted to strike the ball consecutively, passing it among their own players, before returning it over the net?

17. How many points are awarded for a field goal in basketball?

18. Which of the martial arts has a Japanese name that literally means "empty hand"?

19. The Royal and Ancient, in the city of St. Andrews on the east coast of Scotland, is a significant venue in the history of what sport?

20. In inches, what is the diameter of a basketball hoop? 12, 18, 24, or 30?

# Answers

1.  Boston Red Sox.
2.  Four.
3.  Australian Open.
4.  The 1920s.
5.  Skiing.
6.  Curveballs.
7.  22.
8.  The players were on strike.
9.  Biathlon.
10. Swimming.
11. Swiss.
12. Hail Mary.
13. Bandy.
14. Germany.
15. Uruguay.
16. Three.
17. Two.
18. Karate.
19. Golf.
20. 18.

# MOONWALKING

## Timeline of moonwalking astronauts

To date, more than 500 astronauts from three dozen countries have been sent into space—but only 12 human beings in history have ever actually set foot on the Moon. Here, in chronological order, is a full list of all our moonwalkers.

1. NEIL ARMSTRONG
2. BUZZ ALDRIN

*Apollo 11*'s lunar module, the *Eagle*, landed on the surface of the Moon at 8:17 p.m. (UTC) on July 20, 1969. Just over six hours later, at 2:56 a.m. on July 21, Neil Armstrong became the first human being to set foot on the Moon, with the famous words, "That's one small step for man, one giant leap for mankind." Buzz Aldrin followed him just seconds later, and the two men wandered the lunar surface for a total of two hours, 31 minutes, and 40 seconds. *Apollo 11* pilot Michael Collins remained aboard the command module *Columbia* while Armstrong and Aldrin were on the Moon, before later reuniting with them and returning to Earth after a total of eight days in space.

3. PETE CONRAD
4. ALAN BEAN

The third and fourth moonwalkers in history were *Apollo 12* astronauts Pete Conrad and Alan Bean, who made two journeys out onto the lunar surface on November 19 and November 20, 1969. In total, they spent just under eight hours exploring the Moon, during which time they took rock samples, recorded data—and accidentally destroyed a color television camera by pointing it directly at the Sun. For the remainder of their moonwalks, all communication ultimately had to be carried out via radio only.

5. ALAN SHEPARD
6. EDGAR MITCHELL

After the failure of the *Apollo 13* mission, the next moonwalkers were two of the crew of *Apollo 14*, Alan Shepard and Edgar Mitchell. They likewise carried out two moonwalks during their lunar exploration on February 5 and February 6, 1971. Spending more than nine hours on the lunar surface, the pair trekked more than a mile to the edge of a nearby crater—and even found time to hit a few golf balls around!

7. DAVID SCOTT
8. JAMES IRWIN

*Apollo 15* astronauts David Scott and James Irwin carried out three moonwalks over three days on the lunar surface, on July 31, August 1, and August 2, 1971. In total, they spent some 18 hours on moonwalks, becoming the first team to use a motorized Lunar Rover—equipped with a television camera, beaming live video footage back to Houston—to explore more of the surface of the Moon than ever before. In total, they drove across 15.2 miles of lunar terrain, during which time, they recovered a rock sample—code name 15415—estimated to be some 4.5 billion years old. Almost as old as the Moon itself, the rock is now the oldest sample ever returned by an *Apollo* mission, and has since become known as "Genesis Rock."

9.   JOHN YOUNG
10.  CHARLES DUKE

*Apollo 16* astronauts John Young and Charles Duke set the land speed record for the lunar surface during the last of their three moonwalks, undertaken on three successive days from April 21-23, 1972. Driving across the lunar surface to the edge of North Ray Crater, they clocked a maximum speed of 10.5mph.

11.  EUGENE CERNAN
12.  HARRISON SCHMIDT

Eugene Cernan became the last person, to date, to set foot on the Moon when he and fellow *Apollo 17* astronaut Harrison Schmidt completed the third and last of their three moonwalks, December 11–13, 1972. The *Apollo 17* team also spent longer on the Moon than any of their predecessors: Despite their first moonwalk having to be cut short due to time constraints, in total the duo spent just over 22 hours on the lunar surface. At seven hours, 36 minutes and 56 seconds, the second of their three moonwalks is also the longest in history.

# ONLY THE NAMES CHANGE

## Former names of famous bands

Before they were The Beatles—and long before they became the world's best-selling music group!—they were the Quarrymen, so named because founder member John Lennon attended Quarry Bank High School in Liverpool, England. Here are some other former names of some of pop and rock music's best-known bands and artists.

### BEACH BOYS

Before they were the Beach Boys, they were the Pendletones, a name meant to pay homage to the famous Pendleton Woolen Mills flannel shirts, a look popular among California surfers in the 1960s.

### BLACK SABBATH

One of rock music's most successful heavy metal outfits started out playing blues-rock standards under the name The Polka Tulk Blues Band in 1968 before founder member Tony Iommi uncompromisingly told lead singer Ozzy Osborne that he thought the name was "crap." After a short time performing as

Earth, the band eventually took their name from that of a 19?3
Boris Karloff horror movie.

## BLONDIE

Blondie performed two gigs in August 1974 under the name
Angel and the Snake before changing it two months later.
Supposedly, the new name was chosen because of the tendency
of truck drivers to shout "Hey, Blondie!" at lead singer Debbie
Harry as they drove by.

## BLUE ÖYSTER CULT

Blue Öyster Cult founding members Buck Dharma, Albert
Bouchard, and Allen Lanier started performing and recording
under the somewhat less impressive name of Soft White
Underbelly in the late 1960s. A change of line-up and a raft of
poor reviews forced a rethink, and after a brief period as
Oaxaca, The Stalk-Forrest Group, and then The Santos Sisters,
the group adopted their now-famous name in 1970. While the
original name Soft White Underbelly had been lifted from a
wartime speech by Winston Churchill, the name Blue Öyster
Cult was taken from a poem by band manager and producer
Sandy Pearlman.

## DEF LEPPARD

After lead singer Joe Elliott joined rock group Atomic Mass in
1977, they changed their name to Def Leppard and went on to
become one of the most successful heavy metal bands of the
1980s and 90s. Their single *Love Bites* reached #1 on the
Billboard Hot 100 in 1988.

## EARTH, WIND AND FIRE

Earth, Wind and Fire were founded in Chicago in 1969 by singer-songwriter Maurice White as a jazz trio named The Salty Peppers. After White moved to California, the group added several new members, adopted a new sound, and took on a new name based on three of the four traditional elements in classical astrology.

## GREEN DAY

Founded in California in 1987 by 15-year-old school friends Billie Joe Armstrong and Mike Dirnt, Green Day began life as Sweet Children. The group remained as such for two years until 1989 when they changed their name to avoid confusion with another local band named Sweet Baby. Armstrong later told VH1 that he thought Green Day was "the worst band name in the world"!

## LED ZEPPELIN

Led Zeppelin was originally called The New Yardbirds. Guitarist Jimmy Page had been a former member of legendary English rock act The Yardbirds, and toured several cities in Scandinavia with a new group — under the name The New Yardbirds — in 1968, before a cease-and-desist letter from former Yardbirds founder Chris Dreja forced them to rethink their name. They landed on a pun on the expression "lead balloon": "balloon" was changed to Zeppelin, the name of a type of airship, and the A was dropped from "lead" to avoid people mistakenly pronouncing it "leed."

## MAROON 5

Maroon 5 was originally formed as Kara's Flowers while their four founding members were still in high school in 1994. After lead guitarist James Valentine was asked to join the band—transforming them from a fourpiece into a five piece—they changed their name and have recorded as Maroon 5 since 2001.

## PINK FLOYD

At various points in their early history, the English prog-rock group Pink Floyd went by the names Sigma 6, The Meggadeaths, The Screaming Abdabs, Leonard's Lodgers, and Spectrum Five, before settling on the unusual name Tea Set (in honor of their usual rehearsal space in the tearoom of their polytechnic college in London). Luckily, in 1965, the band took on one more change and became Pink Floyd—a combination of the names of blues musicians Pink Anderson and Floyd Council.

## RADIOHEAD

English rock group Radiohead was originally named On A Friday, in honor of their tendency to book rehearsal rooms at the end of the week.

## RED HOT CHILI PEPPERS

The band that eventually became the Red Hot Chili Peppers played two gigs under the name "Tony Flow and the Miraculously Majestic Masters of Mayhem" in February 1983.

## VAN HALEN

Eddie Van Halen's band started under the name Genesis. When Phil Collins' rock group Genesis began to become better known, the band changed their name to Mammoth before finally landing on Van Halen in 1974.

# GETTING SHADY

## Little known names of colors

There might only be seven colors in the rainbow, but in the dictionary, there are countless more names for all the shades and hues in between. Here are just a few of the color names you might never have come across.

Aureolin (sometimes called Cobalt Yellow) is a pigment sparingly used in oil and watercolor painting. Its color index name is PY40 (40th entry on list of yellow pigments). It was first made in 1848 by Nikolaus Wolfgang Fischer in Breslau and its chemical composition is potassium cobaltinitrite.

British racing green, or BRG, is the traditional name given to a rich bottle-green color once widely used on British automobiles.

Carmine is a deep purple-red color, originally made from crushed cochineal beetles. Based on that, the name is thought to derive from an ancient Sanskrit word meaning "worm" or "insect."

Cerise is a bright pinkish-red shade that takes its name from the Latin word for cherry.

Chartreuse is a pale green color, named after the apple-green liqueur of the same name.

Cinnabar is a bright orange-red color. It takes its name from one of the mineral ores of the metal mercury, which is typically an intense brick-red.

Dutch pink, oddly, is a shade of greenish-yellow often found in artists' paint sets.

Gentian is a soft lilac-blue color, named after the gentian flowers typically found in mountain ranges.

Incarnadine is a deep burgundy color. The word means "flesh-colored."

Isabelline is a pale beige, often used in the names of sandy-colored animals and birds. According to legend, its name comes from that of a Spanish infanta named Isabella, who refused to change her crisp white undergarments until her husband was victorious in a siege campaign he was currently waging in Belgium. Unfortunately for Isabella, the siege went on to last for more than 1,000 days—by which time her underclothes was not quite as white as they originally were!

Jonquil is bright yellow. Its name is the French word for the daffodil flower.

Malachite is a rich emerald green color that takes its name from the mineral malachite, one of the main ores of copper.

Mazarine is a rich navy blue. The name is probably derived from that of the Duchesse de Mazarin, a 17th-century noblewoman and a mistress of King Charles II—though how or why she is its inspiration is a complete mystery.

Mignonette is a light grayish-green color, named for the pale-colored leaves of the mignonette plant.

Nacarat is a pale peach-orange. The name is from French but was originally Arabic and is thought to mean "hollowed out" —a reference to the color being like that found on the insides of seashells.

Saxe is a slate gray color, named after the German region of Saxony where dyes of this color were once produced.

Viridian is a rich bluish-green. Supposedly the color of lush vegetation, it derives from a Latin word meaning "to sprout."

Zaffre is a rich dark blue color. It derives from the Arabic name for sapphire.

*"Color is a power which directly influences the soul."*

**Wassily Kandinsky**

# ISLAND LIFE

## World Islands

Although Australia is often claimed to be the world's largest island, geographically it is classified as a "continental landmass." So, at 822,000 square miles—that's only around one-third of Australia's size—Greenland holds the title of the world's largest island. Here are some more facts and figures about the islands of the world.

Madagascar is believed to be the world's oldest island. It split from its nearest continental landmass around 100 million years ago.

Madagascar is also the world's largest independent island nation.

Despite being more than 21,000 square miles in size, Devon Island in the Canadian Arctic is the largest entirely uninhabited island in the world.

Despite its proximity to Canada, Greenland is officially part of the Kingdom of Denmark. If its area were included in official figures, then Denmark would become the 12th largest country in the world—larger even than Saudi Arabia, South Africa, and Mexico.

The island of New Guinea is home to more than 850 different languages.

Discovered in 1739, Bouvet Island in the South Atlantic Ocean is the world's most remote island. It lies 1,400 nautical miles from its nearest neighbor.

With a population of no more than 50, Pitcairn Island is the most remote island in the world, located 3,240 miles (5,215 km) from the coast of New Zealand. The island is inhabited by the descendants of sailors from the HMS Bounty, a Royal Navy vessel that was the scene of a mutiny in 1789. In 2004, the island drew international attention when several of its inhabitants were charged with sexual offences.

Of all the nations in the world, Sweden contains the most islands — more than Greece, the Philippines, Canada, and even Indonesia. Incredibly, Swedish territory encompasses more than 221,000 islands. Even the capital city, Stockholm, is spread across 14 individual islets.

The world's most populous island is Java, Indonesia. It is home to over 141 million people.

If Australia were classed as an island, it would not only be the world's largest but would be a contender for the world's most sparsely populated. It is so vast that despite being home to some 25 million people, Australia has an average population density of just eight people per square mile.

When a volcano erupted on the tiny British-owned island of Tristan da Cunha in the South Atlantic Ocean in 1961, the entire population was evacuated to England.

Bishop Rock in the Scilly Island group in the far southwest of England is home to a single lighthouse erected in 1858. It is said to be the world's smallest island with a building on it.

The largest island in the United States is Big Island, Hawaii.

The most populous island in the United States is Long Island, New York.

On December 29, 2011, the Pacific island nation of Samoa officially switched from one side of the International Date Line to the other. The shift meant that its calendar lost an entire day (there was no December 30, 2011 in Samoa), but it kept its date in line with its nearby trading partners, New Zealand and Australia.

Ilet a Brouee off the south coast of Haiti is just 0.002 square miles in size but is home to 500 people—making it the most densely populated island in the world. Ilet a Brouee is five times more densely populated than Manhattan.

If you were to visit a different Greek island every day, it would take you more than 16 years to visit them all.

Asia's largest island, Borneo, is divided between three different nations: Indonesia, Malaysia, and Brunei. The Bruneian portion of the island is equivalent to just 1% of its entire area.

Victoria Island, which straddles the boundary between Nunavut and the Northwest Territories in the Canadian Arctic, is the eighth-largest island in the world—larger even than Great Britain, Newfoundland, and North Island, New Zealand. In the south of the island, roughly 75 miles from its southern coast, is a long glacial finger lake, in the middle of which is a tiny unnamed island. On that island is an even smaller lake—which is itself home to a tiny sliver of land, barely four acres in size. Due to its inhospitableness and isolation, it's unlikely this tiny four-acre islet has even been visited by human beings, but in 2017 it was granted an extraordinary claim to fame by the *Guinness Book of Records*: It is now officially the largest island in a lake on an island in a lake on an island in the world!

*"Every island to a child is a treasure island."*

**P. D. James**

# POP QUIZ!

## ANIMALS

1. What kind of creature is a hundred-pacer?
2. What would an animal use its "ovipositor" to do?
3. Horseshoe, roundleaf, monkey-faced, and serotine are all types of what nocturnal creature?
4. Where would you likely encounter a wobbegong? Under the sea, in the trees, on a mountainside, or in the Arctic?
5. The world's most venomous creature is often said to be the blue-ringed variety of what creature?
6. Flickers, piculets, and wrynecks are all members of what family of birds?
7. A sleuth is a group of what animals?
8. Spiders have eight legs—but how many eyes do they have?
9. What is a female peacock called?
10. Alligators are only native to two countries globally. The USA—and what other?
11. How many species of venomous snake are found in England?
12. All the world's wild lemurs are found on what African island?
13. A leveret is the young of what creature?

14. What is a female elephant called?
15. Although it's better known as a killer whale, the orca is the world's largest species of what?
16. What kind of creature is a lammergeyer?
17. Apiphobia is the specific fear of what creatures?
18. What animal's name means "nose-horned" in Greek?
19. How many bones are there in a giraffe's neck: 7, 17, 27, or 37?
20. What is the largest cat in the Americas?

# Answers

1. Snake.
2. To lay eggs.
3. Bats.
4. Under the sea (it's a type of shark).
5. Octopus.
6. Woodpeckers.
7. Bears.
8. Eight!
9. Peahen.
10. China.
11. One.
12. Madagascar.
13. Hare.
14. Cow.
15. Dolphin.
16. Vulture.
17. Bees.
18. Rhinoceros.
19. 7.
20. Jaguar.

# NOODLING AROUND

### Pasta

There's an old myth that claims the pasta we know and love today was introduced to Italy by Marco Polo, who brought Chinese noodles back to Europe after traveling the Far East in the 13th century. It's a nice story, but unfortunately, it's probably not true, as pasta was already proving popular in Italy long before his expedition! Nevertheless, here are some definitely true facts and figures about one of our favorite foods.

The word pasta just means "paste" — a reference to the mix of semolina flour and water typically used to make it.

In 2008, Italian chef Francesco Boggian made a record 25 fresh tortellini by hand in just three minutes.

More than 300 different pasta shapes are documented.

Italy produces more than three million tons of pasta every year…

…while on average, an Italian will eat around 60 pounds of pasta in a year!

The earliest known lasagna recipe was published in Europe in the 40th century.

Spaghetti means "little strings."

A single strand of spaghetti is properly called a *spaghetto*.

The longest strand of pasta ever made was 12,388 ft. and 5 inches long. It was cooked in Tokyo in 2010.

Pasta dough is so tough that it was once common to knead it by foot.

World Pasta Day is celebrated on October 25. National Spaghetti Day is January 4.

On April 1, 1957, one of the BBC's flagship current affairs programs, *Panorama*, broadcast a special report about Swiss farmers harvesting a crop of fresh spaghetti from the bushes and trees on their land, and then leaving them to dry in the Alpine sunshine.

Pasta was not particularly widely eaten in England at the time, and so the documentary feature — which was narrated by one of the BBC's most trusted broadcasters, Richard Dimbleby — confused many of the people watching it at home, some of whom wrote to the BBC the following day to ask where they could buy a spaghetti bush of their own. Eventually, of course, it was all revealed to be nothing more than an April Fool's Day hoax!

# ALL THE WORLD'S A STAGE

## Some famous Shakespearean quotes

If you were to read every play, sonnet, and poem written by (or at least credited to) William Shakespeare, you'd have to work your way through nearly 120,000 lines of text and more than 800,000 words—more than 20,000 of which Shakespeare is said to have invented himself. On the way, you'd bypass some of the most famous lines in all of English literature, a few of which are listed here.

"To be, or not to be: that is the question." (*Hamlet*, Act 3, Scene 1)

"All the world's a stage, and all the men and women merely players." (*As You Like It*, Act 2, Scene 7)

"Some are born great, some achieve greatness, and some have greatness thrust upon them." (*Twelfth Night*, Act 2, Scene 5)

"If you prick us, do we not bleed? If you tickle us, do we not laugh?" (*The Merchant of Venice*, Act 3, Scene 1)

"The lady doth protest too much, methinks." (*Hamlet*, Act 3, Scene 2)

"We are such stuff as dreams are made on, and our little life is rounded with a sleep." (*The Tempest*, Act 4, Scene 1)

160

"Beware the Ides of March." (*Julius Caesar*, Act 1, Scene 2)

"The course of true love never did run smooth." (*A Midsummer Night's Dream*, Act 1, Scene 1)

"Lord, what fools these mortals be!" (*A Midsummer Night's Dream*, Act 1, Scene 1)

"A horse! a horse! my kingdom for a horse!" (*Richard III*, Act 5, Scene 4)

"Cry 'havoc!' and let slip the dogs of war." (*Julius Caesar*, Act 3, Scene 1)

"If music be the food of love play on." (*Twelfth Night*, Act 1, Scene 1)

"What's in a name? A rose by any name would smell as sweet." (*Romeo & Juliet*, Act 2, Scene 2)

"The better part of valor is discretion." (*Henry IV: Part 1*, Act 5, Scene 4)

"To thine own self be true." (*Hamlet*, Act 1, Scene 3)

"Neither a borrower nor a lender be." (*Hamlet*, Act 1, Scene 3)

"Off with his head!" (*Richard III*, Act 3, Scene 4)

"Uneasy lies the head that wears the crown." (*Henry IV: Part 2*, Act 3, Scene 1)

"All that glisters is not gold." (*The Merchant of Venice*, Act 2, Scene 7)*

"Friends, Romans, countrymen, lend me your ears: I come to bury Caesar, not to praise him." (*Julius Caesar*, Act 3, Scene 2)

"Brevity is the soul of wit." (*Hamlet*, Act 2, Scene 2)

"What light through yonder window breaks." (*Romeo and Juliet*, Act 2, Scene 2)

"Shall I compare thee to a summer's day?" (Sonnet 18)

* Yes, the original word here is "glisters," not "glitters," as this line is best remembered today!

# THE WORLD'S DEADLIEST ANIMALS

| | Cause of death | Estimated no. fatalities per year |
|---|---|---|
| 1. Mosquitos | Bites, carrying malarial infection | 750,000– 1,000,000+ |
| 2. Snakes | Venomous bites | 50,000–100,000 |
| 3. Dogs | Injury; infected bites | 25,000–35,000 |
| 4. Freshwater snails | Infection via parasite | 10 |
| 5. Assassin bugs | Infectious disease | 10 |
| 6. Tsetse flies | Sleeping sickness | 10 |
| 7. Roundworms | Intestinal infestation | 2,5 |
| 8. Tapeworms | Intestinal infestation | 2 |
| 9. Crocodiles | Predatory attack | 1 |
| 10. Hippopotamuses | Defensive attack | 500–1,000 |

Mortality figures like these are always difficult to judge, as many animal-related deaths occur in remote areas, among isolated peoples and communities, and in countries where such data often goes unreported. The figures here were compiled by the Bill Gates Foundation using WHO data in 2014 as part of their research into worldwide malarial infections.

Many of the creatures listed here are not themselves dangerous but carry infections that can prove fatal if left untreated.

Besides malaria (mosquitos) and rabies (dog bites), freshwater snails carry parasitic worms that can give people a disease called schistosomiasis; assassin bug bites cause a condition called Chagas disease; sleeping sickness is spread by the African tsetse fly; aschariasis, a condition that affects the small intestine, is caused by roundworms; and tapeworms cause a potentially fatal condition called cysticerosis.

Of the world's 200 or so venomous snakes, the saw-scaled viper of India and the Middle East is said to be responsible from anywhere from 60–90% of all snake-bite related deaths per year.

Directly responsible for almost half a million deaths per year, if humans were included on this list, they would be listed second.

Despite being vegetarian, the hippo is Africa's most dangerous animal, responsible for anywhere up to 1,000 deaths every year. Crocodiles rank higher here largely because they are found across a greater area of the world.

Just outside the Top 10 are elephants and lions (both responsible for approximately 100 deaths per year) — while even further outside are such creatures as wolves (ten deaths per year) and sharks (six per year), proving that they're perhaps not as ferocious as we might think!

# IN THE BAG

## Marsupials

Marsupials are a bizarre family of creatures found across Australasia and the Americas, the majority of which carry their young in anatomical pouches. It is from this pouch—properly called a *marsupium*—that the entire marsupial family takes its name. Here are some of the most extraordinary facts and figures about this most curious group of animals.

There are over 300 different species of marsupial, the majority of which are found in Australia and the islands of the Pacific Ocean.

The largest of all marsupials is the red kangaroo of Australia, which can stand as tall as 6 ft. and weigh up to 200 lbs.

The world's smallest marsupial is the Australian long-tailed planigale—a tiny, nocturnal creature measuring just 2.5 inches and weighing less than one-fifth of an ounce.

The largest marsupial that ever lived was Diprotodon, a giant SUV-sized wombat that once inhabited much of Australia.

Marsupials' young are typically born so early in their development that their eyes, ears, and rear limbs often develop after birth in their mothers' pouch.

165

The Virginia opossum is the only species of marsupial in North America.

The Tasmanian tiger or thylacine is believed to have become extinct when the last known individual died in a zoo in the 1930s — but occasional sightings have been made in the wilds of southern Australia in the decades since.

The thylacine is believed to have had the largest bite size of any creature: their jaws could open to an incredible 80°.

Although, usually, it is only the female marsupial that has a pouch, both male and female water opossums do.

Kangaroos can't walk backward.

A male kangaroo is called a boomer, a female kangaroo is called a flyer, and a baby kangaroo is called a joey.

When the Australian Outback becomes too hot, kangaroos cool down by licking their forearms. As the saliva evaporates, it cools the blood under the surface of their skin.

An adult koala can eat more than 2 lbs. of eucalyptus leaves in a single day.

The name *koala* is thought to derive from a word from an Aboriginal language that means "no drink."

Koalas sleep for three-quarters of the day.

# ROLL OVER!

## Beethoven

Ludwig van Beethoven was born in the city of Bonn in western Germany in 1770. In the 56 years of his life, he wrote over 700 pieces of music, among them the famous *Moonlight* sonata, the piano miniature *Für Elise*, and his famous *5th Symphony*. But for all of his extraordinary achievements, few people know much about his life and work — besides the fact that he was for the final years of his life deaf! Here are some more facts and figures about one of music's most famous and celebrated characters.

Beethoven's birthday is believed to be December 16, 1770, given that he was baptized on December 17 and it was typical at that time for baptisms to take place within 24 hours of a child being born. But no one — including Beethoven himself! — actually knows the exact date of his birth.

Beethoven's grandfather was also a musician — and was also called Ludwig van Beethoven!

Beethoven's first music teacher was his father, Johann.

Beethoven was not deaf his entire life: He ascribed his steady hearing loss to a seizure he suffered after quarreling with an opera singer in 1798. Hearing problems plagued him for the next two decades, and he was finally forced to give up public appearances and performances in 1814.

As his deafness worsened, Beethoven was forced to compose at his piano while holding a pencil or a metal rod between his teeth, and rest the opposite end of it on the piano lid. The technique would amplify the sound of the piano via the bones in his jaw.

Some of the medical techniques Beethoven tried to treat his hearing loss included earplugs soaked in almond oil, leeches and bloodletting, daily baths in medicated Danube river water, and galvanism — a new technique at the time in which mild electric currents were passed harmlessly through the afflicted body part.

Beethoven was mistaken for a tramp and arrested in the city of Baden in Germany in 1820. Having been drinking all day, Beethoven was found stumbling around the streets looking for a place to eat, staring through the windows of shops and houses. He was thrown in prison — despite protesting that he was one of the greatest composers in Europe!

No one knows who the "Elise" to whom Beethoven dedicated his famous *Für Elise* piano piece was. One theory is that she was the 19-year-old niece of his doctor, who he proposed to in 1810. (She rejected his advances.)

Beethoven's typical daily working regimen involved cold baths, long afternoon walks that often lasted late into the evening, and a sound night's sleep.

The third-largest crater on the planet Mercury is named in his honor.

At the premiere of his final *9th Symphony* in Vienna in 1824, Beethoven had to be turned around by members of his orchestra to see the rapturous response of the audience. He received five standing ovations—and there are even reports that the applause went on so long it had to be ended by police.

Beethoven's conducting style was dramatic. One observer once commented that he stood on the podium in front of the orchestra and "threw himself back and forth like a madman," and "flailed about with his hands and feet as though he wanted to play all the instruments and sing all the chorus parts."

Beethoven was once challenged to an improvisation contest by a pianist named Daniel Steibelt. Beethoven began by taking a piece of Steibelt's music, placing it upside down on the piano stand, and improvising on its tune for the next hour. Knowing he had been beaten, Steibelt reportedly left the performance before Beethoven had even finished.

Beethoven only wrote one violin concerto, his *Concerto in D major* (Op. 61), which he completed in 1806. Beethoven completed the piece on the night of its very first performance in Vienna—leaving the soloist, acclaimed violinist Franz Clement, very little time to rehearse and rely solely on sight-reading the scribbled manuscript in front of the live audience at its premiere. Perhaps as a result, the performance was not a great success and the piece was seldom performed again in Beethoven's lifetime.

One account claims that Clement was so frustrated by Beethoven's lack of preparation that he interrupted the concerto's two movements with a bravura solo performance of his own invention — played entirely on a single violin string while holding his violin upside down! It seems likely that Clement was trying to demonstrate to the audience (and to Beethoven) that the night's shambolic performance was not caused by his own lack of skill or talent!

Beethoven's last words are claimed to have been, "I shall hear in heaven."

# FIRST PETS

## Timeline of Presidential pets

Only two presidents in American history have not kept pets during their time in the White House: James K Polk and Donald Trump, who is the first president not to own a pet since 1849. Here then are the names and stories behind some of the White House's smallest and furriest inhabitants!

### GEORGE WASHINGTON

George Washington never actually lived at the White House, but work on it began during his presidency in the late 1700s. During that time, Washington kept a great many animals, including American foxhounds named Sweetlips, Scentwell, and Vulcan; a greyhound named Cornwallis; and horses called Nelson, Samson, Steady, and Magnolia. He also had a pet donkey called Royal Gift (so named because he was presented to Washington by the king of Spain), while his wife Martha kept a parrot named Snipe.

### THOMAS JEFFERSON

Jefferson famously kept several mockingbirds during his time in office, of which his personal favorite was a bird named Dick.

He also kept two dogs named Bergère and Grizzle, a horse named Caractacus, and was gifted a male and female pair of bear cubs by Captain Zebulon Pike. Writing that he thought the bears were "too dangerous and troublesome for me to keep," Jefferson gave them to a museum in Philadelphia.

## JAMES MADISON and ANDREW JACKSON

President Madison's only pet was a parrot named Polly, who eventually outlived both him and his wife, Dolley. Andrew Jackson also owned a parrot named Poll, or Polly, during his time in the White House—which famously had quite a robust vocabulary of curse words. Reportedly, the parrot was brought to President Jackson's funeral in 1845 but had to be removed from the ceremony because it would not stop squawking swear words!

## JAMES BUCHANAN

As well as a Newfoundland dog named Lara and a toy terrier called Punch, James Buchanan kept perhaps one of the most impressive presidential pets in history: an eagle.

## ABRAHAM LINCOLN

Abraham Lincoln kept a great many animals throughout his life, including a pair of goats named Nanny and Nanko, dogs called Fido and Jip, a horse called Old Bob, a pair of cats named Tabby and Dixie, and a turkey called Jack (who was originally intended to be eaten for Christmas dinner one year). Lincoln once quipped that his pet cat Dixie was smarter than his entire cabinet.

## RUTHERFORD B. HAYES

President Hayes kept a great many cats and dogs, including a cocker spaniel called Dot; a Newfoundland called Hector; Duke, an English mastiff; a greyhound called Grim; Otis, a miniature schnauzer; a pair of hunting hounds called Juno and Shep; a cat called Piccolomini; and a pair of Siamese cats — the first in the United States — named Siam and Pussy.

## BENJAMIN HARRISON

Besides a collie dog named Dash, Benjamin Harrison is said to have kept a pair of alligators in a greenhouse at the White House. He also had two pet opossums, which he named Mr. Reciprocity and Mr. Protection in honor of the Republican Party's platform slogan during his presidency.

## THEODORE ROOSEVELT

Teddy Roosevelt kept perhaps more pets than any president in history, including countless horses, dogs, chickens, and other birds. Among the strangest additions to his presidential menagerie were several guinea pigs named Admiral Dewey, Bishop Doane, Dr. Johnson, Father O'Grady, and Fighting Bob Evans; a black bear called Jonathan Edwards; an unnamed one-legged cockerel; a hyena named Bill that was a gift from the Emperor of Ethiopia; and a rabbit called Peter Rabbit (who, according to a letter of 1904, was given a full state funeral in the White House grounds). He also had a pet garter snake, which his daughter Alice chose to name Emily Spinach.

## CALVIN COOLIDGE

Calvin Coolidge kept almost as many pets as President Roosevelt had before him, and many were just as bizarre as his predecessor's. Among those President Coolidge kept at the White House were a pair of canaries called Nip and Tuck; a Shetland sheepdog called Calamity Jane; a pair of lion cubs the president named Tax Reduction and Budget Bureau; a family of ducklings that were raised for a time in one of the White House bathrooms; a goose named Enoch; and a pygmy hippopotamus that Coolidge named William Johnson Hippopotamus — or Billy for short!

*"If you want a friend in Washington? Get a dog."*

**Harry Truman**

# POP QUIZ!

## GEOGRAPHY

1.  The Atacama Desert is the largest desert on what continent?
2.  What British city stands at the mouth of the River Clyde?
3.  What U.S. state is bordered by Montana, Wyoming, Nevada, Utah, Washington, Oregon, and Canada?
4.  Name one of the two landlocked countries in South America.
5.  What is the northernmost of Mexico's 31 states?
6.  What is the name of the tiny Alpine nation sandwiched between Switzerland and Austria?
7.  What is the capital city of Ukraine?
8.  In what Canadian body of water do Southampton Island, Coats Island, and Mantel Island lie?
9.  What island nation is separated from mainland India by a stretch of water called the Polk Strait?
10. What is the only African nation whose name begins with K?
11. Sardinia and Sicily are part of what country?
12. On what European sea does the major port of Dubrovnik stand? The Black, the Baltic, the Adriatic, or the Aegean?

13. What is the only U.S. state capital whose name begins with an F?

14. Winnipeg, Brandon, Selkirk, and Steinbach are cities in what Canadian province?

15. The island of Spitsbergen in the vast Svalbard archipelago in the high Arctic is a constituent part of what European country?

16. The Sargasso Sea is a region of what ocean?

17. Peking is the former name of what Chinese city?

18. Normandy, Brittany, and Aquitaine are regions of what country?

19. What country occupies a narrow stretch of land along the west coast of South America, sandwiched between the Andes mountains and the Pacific Ocean?

20. Antananarivo is the capital city of what island?

# Answers

1. South America.
2. Glasgow.
3. Idaho.
4. Bolivia or Paraguay.
5. Baja California.
6. Liechtenstein.
7. Kiev.
8. Hudson Bay.
9. Sri Lanka.
10. Kenya.
11. Italy.
12. Adriatic.
13. Frankfort, Kentucky.
14. Manitoba.
15. Norway.
16. Atlantic.
17. Beijing.
18. France.
19. Chile.
20. Madagascar.

# MAD MONARCHS

## Timeline of mad kings and queens

Think of mad monarchs from history, and you're probably reminded of *The Madness of King George*, the true story of the deranged English King George III that was famously adapted for the big screen in 1994. But poor King George was not the only monarch in history to struggle to keep his sanity. Here are some more of history's (allegedly!) maddest monarchs.

### CALIGULA

The Roman emperor Caligula is well known for the bizarre decisions and sadistic practices he carried out during his rule from 12-41 CE. Famously, the emperor built a lavish palace for his favorite horse Incitatus, had his army construct a vast two-mile floating bridge for him to gallop along, and tried to have his horse appointed to the office of Roman consul. Alas, his plan never came to fruition—Caligula was assassinated before he could see it through.

### CHARLES VI of FRANCE

Known as *Charles le Fou* or "Charles the Mad", Charles VI ruled the kingdom of France for over 40 years, from 1380-

1422. Throughout that time, he suffered many episodes of frenzied psychosis and madness including one of the most damaging bouts in 1393 when King Charles not only forgot his name but forgot that he was the king. Entrances and windows in his Paris residence had to be barricaded up for fear that he might run through them and escape in one of his fits of madness, and in 1405 he suddenly took fright of water and refused to bathe for the next five months. The King also famously suffered from a so-called "glass delusion," believing that his own body was made from fragile glass and that he could shatter to pieces at any moment.

## HENRY VI

The English King Henry VI ascended to the throne while still just an infant in 1421 and reigned intermittently for the next five decades. Toward the end of his reign, however, Henry fell into intense bouts of melancholic lethargy and, in 1453, he suffered such an intense mental breakdown that he slipped into a stupor and did not speak for the following year. Deposed in 1461, he fled into exile in Scotland before being briefly restored to the throne — despite his worsening mental state — in 1470. He passed away the following year.

## RUDOLF II, HOLY ROMAN EMPEROR

Rudolf II ruled Europe's Holy Roman Empire from 1552–1612, during which time his insatiable curiosity for anything and everything led to him becoming one of the greatest patrons of the arts and sciences in Europe's history — as well as one of its most eccentric and obsessive collectors. Rudolf's wild imagination led to his many palaces and residences becoming cabinets of curiosities, stuffed full of artifacts and trinkets from all over the world. Their gardens became menageries, home to wild cats, apes, an orangutan, and even a live dodo bird. However, the emperor's wild flights of fancy were punctuated by mood swings and intense bouts of melancholy that often led to him withdrawing from his court and his royal duties for weeks on end or spending long periods in depressive silence.

## LUDWIG II of BAVARIA

King Ludwig II ruled over Bavaria in Germany from 1845–86. He was another of Europe's great royal patrons of the arts and financed many of the wild projects and compositions of the composer Richard Wagner. The King also funded the construction of many elaborate fairytale-style castles across Bavaria, but as his grand projects became ever wilder and more extravagant—and began to risk bankrupting his kingdom—his advisors had him declared unfit to reign and started making moves to have him deposed. The day after the King's physicians declared him unfit, however, his body was found floating in a lake beside one of his palaces. The cause of his sudden disappearance and death remains unsolved to this day.

# PLACES OF WORSHIP

## World churches and temples

The Basilica of St. Peter in the Vatican City, Rome is said to be the world's largest purpose-built church, capable of holding more than 60,000 worshippers and covering a combined area, inside and out, of more than 43,000 square yards—equivalent to more than eight American football pitches! Here are some more facts about some of the world's most extraordinary churches, temples, and places of worship.

The Temple of the Tooth is the name of a Buddhist temple in Sri Lanka, southern Asia. It is said to house one of the Buddha's teeth.

In parts of Ancient Egypt, there were "sleep temples" where people suffering illness could go and listen to endless hypnotic chanting to lull them to sleep and help their recovery.

Cross Island Chapel, a non-denominational church on Mason's Pond in Oneida, New York, is said to be the smallest church in America. Erected in 1989, it is just 4 ft., 3inches x 6 ft., 9 inches in size.

The oldest surviving Christian church is said to be a converted house that originally stood in Qal'at es Salihiye, Syria. Constructed sometime around 232 CE, in the 1930s it was dismantled by archaeologists and rebuilt back in the United States.

Seoul, the capital city of Korea, is home to the world's largest underground church. SaRang Church (South Korea), with a total floor space of 8,418 m² (90,610 ft.) that is spread across 7 main chapels and sanctuaries and can accommodate 9,380 seated people.

The bells of St. Lawrence's Church in Ipswich, England, were cast in 1440. They are the oldest church bells known to still be in use today.

According to the *Guinness Book of Records*, a 100-capacity church building in Chinese Taipei is the world's largest building shaped like a shoe.

With a 530 ft. central steeple, Ulm Minster in southern Germany is the tallest church in the world — and the fifth-tallest structure built before the 20th century.

The Catalan architect Antoni Gaudí's design for the Sagrada Família church in Barcelona, Spain, is so complex that when Gaudí died in 1926, only a quarter of the project had been completed after 44 years' work. The church was finally consecrated by Pope Benedict XVI in 2009 but is still not due to be completed until 2030-40.

There is a wooden ladder in the Church of the Holy Sepulcher in Jerusalem that has stood in the same place since 1728 because removing it would involve consultation and agreement between the leaders of all six Christian denominations who claim ownership of the church.

Every single part of the Church of the Transfiguration on Kizhi Island in western Russia is made entirely of wood.

A set of beehives, home to more than 100,000 bees, installed on the roof of the Notre Dame church in Paris survived the fire that destroyed much of the rest of the building in 2019.

The most-visited religious building in the world is said to be the Tirupati Hindu Temple in the city of Tirupati in southern India. It welcomes anywhere from 30,000 to 75,000 worshippers every day.

In Caracas, Venezuela, it is traditional to roller-skate to church on Christmas morning.

The world's largest prayer wheel was built in Gansu, China, in 2018. The wheel measured 26.285 m (86 ft. 2.84 in) in height and 10.22 m (33 ft. 6.36 in) in diameter, and weighed 200 tons (440.9245 lb.).

*"The day we find the perfect church, it becomes imperfect the moment we join it."*

**Charles H. Spurgeon**

# 10 MOST COMMONLY MISSPELLED WORDS

1. Separate
2. Zucchini
3. Questionnaire
4. Potato
5. Diarrhea
6. Definitely
7. Embarrass
8. Conscience
9. Unnecessary
10. Bureaucracy

This list is based on data from a 2020 survey by Google, who looked at the words most frequently typed incorrectly into their online search bar.

Separate tops this list, with its most common misspelling — in which its middle A is replaced with an E, *separate* — being typed into Google some 92,000 times in one month.

Elsewhere, it seems double letters are a common cause of English spelling troubles, with the likes of *zucchini, questionnaire*, and *unnecessary* all making the top 10.

# FAVORITE HAUNTS

## Stories behind famous haunted houses

The so-called Winchester Mystery House, a mansion house in San Jose, California, is famously said to be one of the most haunted houses in America. The former home of Sarah Winchester—the widow of firearm magnate William Wirt Winchester—legend has it that Sarah demanded the house be continually built and extended to appease the spirits of all those killed by her husband's weaponry. Although it remains debatable how true that legend is, of course, the house has nevertheless become famous for its many resident ghosts and apparent hauntings—as have all the buildings and structures listed here.

## LALAURIE MANSION

Part of the inspiration for the spooky television series *American Horror Story: Coven*, the LaLaurie Mansion in New Orleans was once home to a murderous socialite named Madame Marie Delphine LaLaurie in the early 1800s. While holding glitzy parties for her high-society guests downstairs, LaLaurie would murder people upstairs. The grotesque truth was only discovered when a fire broke out in the kitchen of the grand townhouse in 1834, after which LaLaurie is believed to have fled to Europe. Today, the house is thought to be haunted by countless spirits including many of LaLaurie's victims — and, according to legend, Madame LaLaurie herself.

## BORLEY RECTORY

Although it was destroyed by fire in 1939 and was pulled down in 1944, Borley Rectory in the village of Borley in Essex, England, is said to have been the most haunted house in Britain. Built in the mid-1800s, over the 100 years that it stood in the village, the house's inhabitants reported hearing distant footsteps and ringing servants' bells; seeing visions of a ghostly nun who haunted its grounds; and even witnessing a ghostly horse-drawn carriage driven by a headless driver pulling up outside. But perhaps creepiest of all the incidents that plagued the house was one very real yet unexplained discovery: In 1927, the wife of the house's owner at the time, the Reverend Guy Smith, found a brown paper package at the back of a disused cupboard that contained nothing more than a young woman's skull.

## RMS *QUEEN MARY*

Although not a strictly speaking a house, the long and eventful history of the luxury ocean liner RMS *Queen Mary* has still made it one of the most haunted locations in America. Originally launched in 1936, during World War II, the liner was stripped of many of its lush interiors and repurposed as a military troopship; Prime Minister Winston Churchill famously signed the D-Day declaration aboard the *Queen Mary* in 1944. After the war, the ship's luxurious interior was restored, and it resumed its life as a grand cruise liner for the rich and famous until it was retired and permanently docked off Long Beach, California. Used as a floating hotel and restaurant today, the ship is said to be haunted by the ghosts of many of the crew members and soldiers who died on board during its long service—as well as an anonymous passenger who was apparently brutally murdered in cabin B340 in the 1960s.

## THE STANLEY HOTEL

The splendid Stanley Hotel in Estes Park, Colorado, was built in 1909—and decades later, apparently inspired Stephen King's macabre tale of a haunted hotel, *The Shining*. Said to be haunted by the ghosts of its original owners and architects, at the Stanley, bags are often reportedly mysteriously packed and unpacked, pianos play themselves, unexplained knocks and footsteps are heard inside locked rooms, and disembodied children's laughter is said to echo down the hallways.

## THE MONTE CRISTO HISTORIC HOMESTEAD

The Monte Cristo estate in the town of Junee, New South Wales, is said to be Australia's most haunted building. A late Victorian mansion house, among the many spirits said to reside in the Monte Cristo are the ghost of a stable boy who burnt to death in a tragic accident, a young child who died falling down one of the house's grand staircases, a maid who fell from a balcony, and the young son of one of the house's caretakers, who was once discovered lying beside the dead body of his mother in mysterious circumstances.

# POP QUIZ!

## POT LUCK

1. Robert Crawley, the Earl of Grantham, and Violet Crawley, the Dowager Countess of Grantham, were characters in what period drama series?
2. Who has been editor-in-chief of *Vogue* magazine since 1988?
3. The resorts of Valencia, Málaga, and Benidorm are in what European country?
4. Which of these sports competitions is the oldest: the French Open, the Super Bowl, the FIFA World Cup, or the Kentucky Derby?
5. What kind of item of clothing is an "Oxford bag"?
6. In the English language version of *Scrabble*, what two tiles are valued at ten points?
7. The criminal Abel Magwitch and the mysterious Miss Havisham are characters in what Charles Dickens novel?
8. Gary Oldman won the 2019 Best Actor Academy Award for his portrayal of which historical figure?
9. The soles of which famous fashion designer's shoes are characteristically covered in bright red lacquer?
10. What is 4 cubed?

11. Which pop superstar's albums include *Fearless*, *Speak Now*, and *Lover*?
12. Which English comedian and actor is known for playing Johnny English and Mr. Bean?
13. Which Major League Baseball team is associated with Canada's Rogers Centre?
14. What is the name of the main protagonist in Washington Irving's famous tale *The Legend of Sleepy Hollow*?
15. In 1904, what became the first American city to host the Olympic Games?
16. The roadrunner is the official bird of what U.S. state?
17. Who was the first person to receive ten acting Oscar nominations?
18. If you were born on Veterans Day, what would your star sign be?
19. In medicine, what is a cicatrix?
20. Sun, sloth, and spectacled are the names of species of what large mammal?

# Answers

1.  *Downton Abbey.*
2.  Dame Anna Wintour.
3.  Spain.
4.  Kentucky Derby (1875).
5.  Trousers.
6.  Q and Z.
7.  *Great Expectations.*
8.  Winston Churchill.
9.  Christian Louboutin.
10. 64.
11. Taylor Swift.
12. Rowan Atkinson.
13. Toronto Blue Jays.
14. Ichabod Crane.
15. St Louis.
16. New Mexico.
17. Bette Davis.
18. Scorpio.
19. A scar.
20. Bear.

# AT LAST

## Famous lasts

At his death in Baltimore on November 14, 1832, at the age of 95, Maryland senator Charles Carroll III was the longest-lived of the 59 signatories of the American Declaration of Independence. Incredibly, Carroll had lived another 56 years after signing the document alongside the likes of Thomas Jefferson, Benjamin Franklin, and Benjamin Harrison. Here, finally, are some more of the world's most interesting lasts and finales.

The last dodo bird is believed to have died in 1681.

The last U.S. President not born in a hospital was Lyndon B. Johnson, who was born in a Texas farmhouse in 1908.

Shakespeare's last play was *The Tempest*.

The last word of Shakespeare's last sonnet is "love."

The last song recorded together by The Beatles was *I Me Mine* in 1970.

The last surviving widow of the Revolutionary War was Esther Sumner Damon, who died on November 11, 1906, at the age of 92.

France's last execution by guillotine was in 1977.

Henry Pu-yi was the last emperor of China, ruling from 1908–12.

The last song ever publicly performed by Elvis Presley was *Bridge Over Troubled Water*.

If all the words in a dictionary were spelled backward, the last word in a dictionary would be *muzz*.

Alphabetically, the last country in the world is Zimbabwe. It shares its northern border with the second last, Zambia.

"How do you find your way back in the dark?" was the last line spoken on screen by Marilyn Monroe in her last film, *The Misfits*.

Baseball star Hank Aaron hit his 755th and last home run in Milwaukee on July 20, 1976.

The 1912 Stockholm Olympics were the last Olympic Games where the gold medals were solid gold.

On March 21, 1963, Frank Wathernam became the last prisoner to leave Alcatraz prison.

Anne Frank's last diary entry is dated August 1, 1944.

The last Californian grizzly bear was spotted in the Sierra Mountains in 1924.

The last transatlantic *Concorde* flight landed in London on October 24, 2003.

The last words spoken on the Moon by astronaut Eugene Cernan were, "with peace and hope for all mankind."

Nicholas II was the last czar of Russia. He and his family were executed in 1918.

The last state to repeal Prohibition was Utah, in December 1933.

Pope Adrian II, who reigned from 867 to his death in 872, was the last pope to be married.

The last letter of the Greek alphabet was *omega*.

The last word in the Bible is "amen."

*"Die, my dear? That's the last thing I'll do!"*

**Groucho Marx**

# CONCLUSION

Alas, we've come to the end of our journey through some of the world's weirdest and most wonderful, biggest and smallest, firsts and lasts, and facts and figures.

Along the way, we've been to Ancient Egypt and Shakespeare's London. We've journeyed all around the world and into outer space.

We've met moonwalkers and rock stars, Olympians and Oscar-winners, presidents and prime ministers—and even spent some time in the company of the world's greatest detective!

If you've been with us since page one, hopefully, you're now fully prepared to liven up your next conversation—when the opportunity arises!—with whatever bizarre tidbit of trivia has caught your eye.

Perhaps it's the former name of the Beach Boys? Or the world's tallest waterslide? Or the story of the maddest of mad monarchs? Or maybe you're planning on testing out that theory about filling up the Grand Canyon while shuffling a deck of playing cards...?

Until next time!

# DON'T FORGET YOUR FREE BOOKS

## GET THEM FOR FREE ON
## WWW.TRIVIABILL.COM

# MORE BOOKS BY BILL O'NEILL

I hope you enjoyed this book and learned something new.

Please feel free to check out some of my previous books on
**Amazon**.

Made in the USA
Monee, IL
13 June 2022

97952903R20115